MW01489200

Tiger Island

Jack Ritchie

First Class Publishers
Stevens Point, Wisconsin

Tiger Island

ISBN 0-932310-09-5

Tiger Island

one

Forrest turned his car off the sea road and pulled up behind the collection of weather-beaten buildings at the base of the long wharf.

He studied the half dozen cottages facing the ocean. No, he thought, I don't really remember any of this at all. It doesn't bring back anything.

He carried his suitcases up the dry wooden stairs into Pete's Bar. A steady breeze from the screened windows moved through the low-ceilinged room.

The bartender glanced his way and waited, but Forrest moved on to the only two other people in the room.

They sat waiting at one of the tables, the solidly built man with dark hair beginning to gray, the girl's violet eyes cool and appraising.

Forrest stopped before them. "Mike Hegan?"

Hegan nodded. "And I guess that makes you Forrest?"

They shook hands and Hegan introduced the girl. "This is Eve." He hesitated just a moment. "My daughter."

Eve smiled, but there remained something careful in her eyes, something neutral. She was waiting to learn more about Forrest before she made up her mind about him, one way or the other.

Hegan ordered a drink for Forrest. "It's nice to meet you, but we could have done all of this by mail."

Forrest agreed. "I suppose so, but I wanted to see the island once more before I made up my mind."

Hegan's eyes turned to the ocean-side windows. "You

3

can just make it out from here. How long have you been away?"

"I was seven when my family left for the last time. I remember very little about the place."

But a few more things were coming back now. A few faint memories. The long-maned pony. What was his name? Bobby? The misty island mornings and a voice calling for him. A sharp woman's voice.

Outside, metal drums were being winched into the well of a cabin cruiser moored alongside the wharf.

"Fuel for the generator," Hegan said. "I had my place electrified. Put in plumbing and things like that."

Forrest turned from the window. "I've been told that you already control half of the island. But you want all of it?"

"I'm the kind of a person who likes a whole island. But don't try to hold me up because of that. I can live with half an island if I have to. I think my offer is fair enough."

Forrest nodded. "If I decide to sell."

Eve had been silent until now. "You don't really have to sell?"

"Not if I don't want to." Forrest regarded Hegan. "What do you intend to do with a whole island of your own?"

"I'll develop the place. I've got a few plans, a few surprises."

On the deck of the cruiser, a scowling red-faced man unhooked the winch cable from a drum.

"Jim Pitts," Hegan said. "My caretaker."

Forrest frowned slightly. "Somehow he looks familiar."

"He was born on the island," Hegan said. "But I don't suppose you could call him one of the gentry."

They watched Pitts pull a half pint bottle from his rear pocket and unscrew the cap.

"He's got a few bad habits," Hegan said. "But I need somebody on the island twelve months a year. We spend only six or seven weeks there ourselves. If you don't have somebody watching over the place, word gets around that the island is deserted and people begin using it for a

4

campground."

Forrest tasted his drink. "You're from up north? How did you ever happen to hear about the island?"

"My secretary, Oriana. She lived there until she was eighteen. Just her and her mother in the Deveraux house. The pair of them were the last people on the island. Even Pitts was gone by then and living on the mainland. Oriana left too after her mother died. She sometimes talks about the Forrest plantation. It must have been something of a showplace in its day, wasn't it?"

"Yes."

"She tells me it burned down."

"Yes. Nine years ago."

On the cruiser, Pitts hunkered down in the shade of the cabin and tilted the bottle again.

Hegan snapped his swizzle stick and dropped it into his empty glass. "Did you have peacocks on your plantation?"

"Not that I remember."

Hegan smiled. "I once spent a couple of days at a place like that in South Carolina. Big house. Grounds like a park and those damn peacocks on the front lawn. And white deer and God knows what other kinds of animals. Like a zoo, except that they were all tame and loose. Never could get the place out of my mind."

Hegan looked seaward again. "When I came to the island the Deveraux house was the only building still standing. All the other places were rotted out and gone. Or burnt down. Even the Deveraux place was damn near falling apart. Roof sagging and leaking, most of the windows busted, and everything just about ready to collapse. But I brought in people and they put everything back together again, only better than it ever was. I probably spent ten times more fixing up that house than it cost to build in the first place. I'm even thinking of putting in air-conditioning."

"You shouldn't really need it," Forrest said. "The island houses were built with natural air-conditioning in mind. High ceilings, big rooms and plenty of ventilation."

A dusty taxi drew up in front of the building and a tall

5

balding man clutching a briefcase got out. The driver removed two suitcases from the trunk and waited for his fare.

"That's MacIntyre," Hegan said. "A third cousin or something like that to my wife. Dr. Jamie MacIntyre. And believe it or not, he's an elected coroner. He'll be spending a few days with us on the island."

The cab pulled away leaving MacIntyre beside his suitcases, staring uncertainly at Pete's Bar. He took out his handkerchief and wiped perspiration from his forehead and scalp.

Hegan grinned. "He knows we're in here, but he won't set foot in a place like this. Promised his mother, I guess. He doesn't smoke, drink or swear, so there's got to be something really big wrong with him and some day I'll find out what it is. Let him stand out there in the sun and sweat. He sweats easy, usually cold."

MacIntyre glared at Pete's Bar for a few more seconds, then picked up his suitcases and stalked toward the docked cruiser.

Hegan pushed away his glass. "For some damn reason my wife feels sorry for him or he wouldn't be with us so often." He rose. "We might as well shove off for the island."

At closer range, Forrest found that MacIntyre appeared to be in his early fifties, with a slight stoop, and quite pale. He offered a hand to Forrest and quickly withdrew it after one shake.

He doesn't like to touch people, Forrest thought. Something you don't expect to find in a doctor.

Pitts looked Forrest over slowly and then showed yellowing teeth. "You don't remember me, do you?"

"No."

"I used to work for your father," Pitts said. "For a long time."

Forrest, Eve and MacIntyre went down into the cabin. Outside, the motor throbbed to life and with Hegan at the wheel, the cruiser moved slowly seaward toward the island.

MacIntyre closed his eyes as the craft began responding to the swells. He clutched his briefcase tightly to his chest, his fingers making damp marks on its metal lock.

Eve now smiled at Forrest again. "Has your family always owned half of the island?"

"No. Originally there were twelve plantations."

"I suppose the Civil War ended the good life?"

"For some. Gradually the plantation families gave up, sold out, and moved off the island."

"But not the Forrests?"

"Not the Forrests. They had investments in the North and the war hardly touched their pocketbooks at all. As a matter of fact they were considerably better off after the war than before."

"But eventually they too left the island?"

"Yes." Forrest studied the faint low outline of the island ahead of them. "There are people who love islands and there are people who just think they do. My mother was a New Yorker and after she married my father, she came down here all enthusiastic about settling down on Forrest Plantation. But the enthusiasm wore thin after a while. I suppose it was because of the isolation and the fact that by the time she came here the Forrests were just about the only people still there.

"After a few years, she decided that the plantation wasn't going to be her permanent home anymore. We still returned to the island for a month or two every year, probably as a concession to my father. But then one night while we were in Europe, lightning struck the house and burned it to the ground. My mother was not exactly grief stricken. You either love an island or you begin to hate it."

Hegan turned the wheel over to Pitts and now joined them in the cabin. He eyed MacIntyre. "Jamie doesn't care too much for saltwater. He's trying hard not to think about how the waves go up and down. Up and down. Up and down."

MacIntyre opened his eyes and glared at him.

Hegan lit a cigar, blew some of the smoke in MacIntyre's direction, then turned to Forrest. "People tell me that there are still some alligators on the island."

Forrest now remembered. "Yes. My mother used to

frighten me with stories about the gators in the swamp. I suppose it was her way of keeping me from wandering off too far. The gators aren't native to the island. They were brought in by planters to discourage the slaves from running away and hiding in the swamp. It didn't work out too well. The runaways ate the gators, instead of the other way around. Anyway, the swamp really wasn't the best place to hide. Not big enough, for one thing. Eventually the runaways were faced with the choice of getting caught or trying to swim to the mainland, where things couldn't have been much better. Some of them tried, but as far as anyone knows, no one ever made it."

Hegan smiled faintly. "Henry could make it."

"Henry?"

"My son. Henry. He's a swimming fool. Has all kinds of medals and trophies and badges. He once swam a couple of hundred miles down the Mississippi. Or was it up? I forgot to ask."

As the cruiser neared the island, it made a turn and moved up along its coast. Vegetation grew to the edge of the thin strip of white sand. Behind the beach lay flowering dogwood trees and beyond--a dark forest of live oaks festooned with Spanish moss, mistletoe and wild grapes. The scent of wild oranges lingered in the air.

The craft rounded a bend and came upon a sudden squealing from the shore, and Forrest saw the rush of small animals into the underbrush.

"Pigs," Hegan said. "Wild pigs. Descendants of the domestic ones that got away. They come down to the shore to root up clams. It's their main diet. I shot one once and tried to eat it. Fishy taste. As far as I'm concerned they're not fit to eat. At least not by humans."

A long stone wharf lay ahead, a Buick station wagon parked at its foot.

"In the old days ocean-going schooners could tie up to load and unload right here at the island," Hegan said. "It made things more convenient and independent of the mainland."

The cruiser slowed as Pitts swung the wheel to ease alongside the wharf. He cut the throttle and let the boat glide in. Hegan took care of the mooring chores.

On the dock, they got into the station wagon. Hegan took the wheel. "The house is only a half mile or so from here."

He drove slowly, turning now and then to avoid pot holes in the dirt roadway. "I'll have to get this damn thing paved. I'll be sinking a lot of money into this island. I just hope it pays off, one way or another."

They pulled out of the tunnel of trees and into the clear land before the Deveraux house. It was a long two-and-a-half story structure with upper and lower verandas along its entire length, both front and back.

Hegan stopped the wagon and turned off the ignition. "The first Deverauxs came east from Lousiana in the early 1800s. They evidently liked the kind of houses they had back there, because they built this one. Most of the other places on the island were what they call Federal, with a lot of pillars."

Hegan took one of Forrest's suitcases and led the way. "You'll like my wife. Everybody does. You'll be calling her Laurie after the first five minutes."

two

They went up the wide front stairs to the main floor veranda. Inside the house, in the coolness of one of the large rooms, Laurie Hegan met them.

She's probably just about the same age as her husband, Forrest thought, but time has been more than kind. She looks closer to thirty and she hasn't lost anything. She had wide blue, frank eyes.

Laurie smiled and spoke her welcome and then turned to MacIntyre. "How are you, Jamie?"

He flushed. "Just fine, Laurie."

"Well, I could use a drink," Hegan said, and he moved toward the liquor cabinet. A high-pitched yelp came from the floor and a small black terrier dashed away. He ran to Laurie and cowered at her feet.

"Damn," Hegan said. "I stepped on him. What the hell was he doing under there anyway?"

"Hiding, I think." Laurie regarded the dog with a trace of worry. "He's been huddling under things ever since we got here this time. He even howled like a lost soul a little while ago."

Hegan opened the liquor cabinet. "It's the south wind."

Laurie looked at him. "What's the south wind got to do with it?"

Hegan regarded the shivering dog. "Homely little mutt, isn't he, Mr. Forrest? He followed Laurie home one day and she didn't have the heart to kick him out." He turned to MacIntyre. "She's always adopting things, isn't that right, Jamie?"

10

Laurie spoke to Forrest. "Supper--or I suppose I should call it dinner--will be ready in about an hour. I'll get Bowler to show you up to your room so you can unpack. Jamie, you take your usual room."

Hegan quickly downed a shot of whiskey. "I'll show Forrest up."

He picked up one of Forrest's suitcases again and led the way outside to the stairs at the end of the veranda. MacIntyre followed, having trouble with his own luggage and the briefcase.

"All the stairways are on the outside of the building," Hegan said. "Except for a small one in the back leading down to the service quarters."

He paused at a door on the second floor veranda. "By the way, Forrest, don't leave any loose change lying around. Or bills. Bowler has light fingers."

Behind them, MacIntyre sniffed. "I thought I missed five dollars from my wallet the last time I was here."

Hegan looked him over. "Jamie, why do you hang onto that briefcase so tight every time you come here? What the hell do you keep in there?"

MacIntyre stiffened. "My notes. I'm doing a paper."

"That's nice, Jamie. Seems to me that you're always doing a paper. One of these days I'll have to ask Bowler if that's really true."

"What does Bowler have to do with it?"

"He's got this ring of keys, Jamie. Big keys, little keys, medium-sized keys. And he likes unlocking things. I wouldn't be at all surprised if some day he opens that briefcase. Maybe he already has."

MacIntyre lost color. "I'll kill him if he touches it."

Hegan grinned. "Would you really, Jamie? Kill Bowler? That sounds pretty fierce." He watched MacIntyre disappear into a room further down the wide veranda and then opened the door to Forrest's high-ceilinged bedroom.

"Every room goes the width of the house, so you have both the front and the rear veranda to play with. It makes for a lot of shade...and in this climate you can use all you can get plus plenty of fresh air. Sometimes birds even fly right through the rooms."

11

Hegan tested a light switch. "All electric now. And each bedroom's got a bath. The generator is in a cabin in back of the house. Had the thing installed in the summer kitchen first, but I had to move it farther away because it made too much noise."

Forrest put a suitcase on the bed. "Does he?"

"Does who what?"

"Does Bowler have that ring of keys?"

"Damned if I know. But I wouldn't put it past him."

"You like riding MacIntyre, don't you?"

Hegan smiled. "He brings out the mean streak in me." He watched Forrest snap open the suitcase. "Bowler's not a big-league thief. He works on the percentage basis. He takes as much as he thinks you won't miss--some change here and there, or maybe even a buck or two. Once I left my wallet on the dresser with a twenty dollar bill inside. Just one solid twenty. I wanted to see how Bowler would handle the situation."

"How did he?"

"The next time I picked up the wallet, I found a ten, a five and three ones."

"Why don't you fire him?"

"I would, except that his wife, Clara, pulls up the slack. She knows how to run the house. She'd quit if I got rid of Bowler. Or at least I think so, but you never know. I've been noticing things lately." He moved to the door. "See you at dinner."

When Hegan was gone, Forrest finished unpacking and then stepped out onto the rear veranda. In the gathering dusk he saw a small figure jogging up the back road toward the house.

The slightly-built man slowed to a walk for the last hundred yards and then trotted up the rear stairs. He halted and blinked when he saw Forrest. "You must be Forrest?"

"Yes."

"I'm Henry. Henry Hegan."

Henry appeared to be in his middle twenties and wore dark shell glasses. He shook hands eagerly. "I run ten miles a day. Whenever I have the time and I always have

12

the time. When I'm in training, I do at least twice that. You have to be in shape because fatigue makes cowards of us all."

Forrest took a moment to absorb that. "I understand that you're something of a swimmer? I suppose you do a lot of that here?"

"No. Not here. Not swimming. But I do a lot of running. Along the beaches mostly. There's a road leading inland but it's neglected and hard on my feet." Henry used the sleeve of his sweat shirt to wipe perspiration from his forehead. "I've done research on this island. History, you know."

"Then you probably know a lot more about it than I do, Henry."

Henry agreed readily. "The original settlers came here in 1679. There was even a little town on the island long ago, but most of the people left for one reason or another. The first slaves were brought here in the 1720s." He pushed the bridge of his glasses back up. "Sea Island cotton. That was the economic reason for the island being alive. It had a long fiber that made it prime. Something to do with making it easier or more worthwhile removing the seeds. That was before the cotton gin and everything was hand labor. And being an island, there was never any real trouble with the slaves running away. Permanently, I mean. Or very far. Usually they hid in the swamp or they drowned trying to swim to the mainland. Do you keep in shape?"

"I don't really work at it, Henry."

"I can jog all day long. Have you met the others?"

"I think so."

"Eve's not really my sister. Not my blood, at least. I mean she was adopted by Mike and Laurie. And Laurie's my stepmother. My father's second wife. My real mother died when I was ten. I can explain it all again if you want. Do you like Laurie?"

"Of course."

Henry nodded. "Everybody likes Laurie. Well, practically everybody." He stared off at the woods behind the house. "The trouble with jogging is that you've always got to take a shower afterwards. Sometimes two or three times a day, depending on how many times you decide to jog. And it's dull too."

"The showers are dull?"

"Well, yes. But I meant jogging. Especially at the university field house back home. That's where I do my jogging when we're not here. Just around and around the track. One tenth of a mile. I keep count with beans."

Forrest waited.

"I count out fifty beans when I want to do fifty laps. And after each lap I drop one of the beans into a bucket at the side of the track as I go past."

Henry rubbed his nose. "I don't jog all the way around the island because there are a lot of places where there are just too many bushes and things. I have this measured stretch along the beach and here I use pebbles for counting and I go back and forth, back and forth. I guess I'll take my shower now. This is the third one today."

He moved down the veranda a half dozen steps and then turned. "The reason showers are dull is because they're non-creative. At best, just maintenance. No matter how much you scrub, you really can't get any cleaner than you were yesterday."

Henry disappeared into one of the doorways at the end of the veranda.

Forrest returned to his own room and decided that taking a quick shower wasn't a bad idea. When he finished and dressed, he went downstairs.

Hegan met him on the front veranda and led him into a large room. "This is my den or what have you when I'm on the island." He opened a liquor cabinet and poured bourbon into two glasses. "I thought I heard voices up there a while ago. Was that Henry talking to you?"

"Yes."

Hegan handed Forrest a glass. "Strange kid. Doesn't say a word for six months and then suddenly he'll latch onto someone and begin babbling. Henry's crazy about the island. Spends most of the day out there running along the beach."

Forrest paused before a rifle on a wall rack.

14

"Weatherby .300 Magnum," Hegan said. "I've got quite a collection back home, but this is the only one I've brought down here so far. I'm picking up another Weatherby the next time I stop off at Savannah. Got it on order."

"What is there to hunt on this island?"

"Deer, but I'll admit they're kind of stunted. Then there are the pigs. But they're not much sport. Maybe I'll try my hand at some of the alligators in the swamp."

Forrest remembered. "When I was small, sometimes I could hear them roaring in the night."

"They're still there and I hear them myself now and then."

Forrest became aware of a raven-haired woman standing in the doorway. Her emerald-green eyes seemed faintly hostile.

"I don't think you've met Oriana," Hegan said. "My secretary. Where have you been Oriana?"

"Walking."

He regarded her. "Where?"

"Along the beach. Just along the beach."

At dinner, MacIntyre brought his briefcase to the table. He kept it on the floor beside his foot and touched it every now and then as though to reassure himself that it was still there and locked.

three

It was a little after two in the morning and Forrest had been unable to sleep.

He lay on his bed, his eyes open, listening to the movement of the wind through the leaves of the live oaks outside.

Finally he sighed and rose. He slipped into his slacks and a sport shirt and stepped out onto the rear veranda.

He looked down at the moonlit abandoned back garden and then up and over the dark thickness of the trees beyond. How far away was the old Forrest plantation? When the big house still existed, could you have seen it from here?

He shivered slightly at the cool mist drifting in from the sea as he made his way down the back stairs. He found a garden bench and sat down.

I'll have to see my father's grave while I'm here, he thought, I've got to do at least that.

He glanced back toward the house at the sound of a door being opened and closed. He saw Hegan moving down the length of the second floor veranda and carrying a suitcase.

When Hegan reached ground level, he became aware of Forrest. He moved closer. "Having trouble sleeping?"

Forrest nodded. "I'm beginning to remember things and they're interesting enough to keep me awake."

"I couldn't sleep either," Hegan said. "I turned on the radio and discovered that there's bad weather coming in. I've got a ten o'clock business appointment on the mainland tomorrow and I can't afford to miss it. I was going to cross in the morning, but by then I might not be able to make it at all. So I decided I'd better leave right now."

He indicated his suitcase. "Just in case of an emergency. I hate to get caught on the mainland without an extra shirt if I find I have to stay away longer than I expected." Hegan checked his watch. "I'll have to wake Pitts. He'll ride with me to the wharf and bring back the wagon. He'll need it tomorrow and I think he'd rather lose a little sleep now than have to take a long walk to the wharf tomorrow morning."

Forrest volunteered. "I'll ride along and bring the car back."

They went around the house to the front where the station wagon was parked.

Hegan started the motor and turned on the lights. He followed the winding road through the trees and when he reached the ocean, he drove onto the wharf and stopped beside the berthed cruiser.

Forrest stepped out and studied the horizon. "The fog is moving in fast. Are you sure you can still make it to the mainland?"

"I'll make it."

A faint distant roar came from the island behind them. Forrest turned. "What was that?"

"Probably one of your bull alligators in the swamp."

"I don't think that came from the swamp."

Hegan smiled. "I heard that alligators will walk over land at night when they feel the urge. Maybe one of them is hungry and looking for a meal."

Once Hegan was aboard the cruiser, Forrest cast off the lines. He watched the craft move off and increase speed, the boat's lights flickering in the motion of the sea.

Forrest drove the station wagon back to the house. He returned to his room, undressed and lay down on the bed again.

Once more he heard the faint roar. He sat up, listening, waiting for the sound to be repeated, but it was not.

Eventually Forrest drifted into sleep and dreams....

The gator had been shot in the swamp and brought

back to one of the old slave cabins at the Forrest place. The cook had told him and Forrest had run out of the big house to get a look.

The gator had been lying in the short grass on its back and Forrest had walked around the body. His father, his mother and Miss Lockey had all told him how big the gators were. As long as a room or longer and fierce.

But this one wasn't big at all. Maybe as long as a man was tall, but no more than that and Forrest had been disappointed.

He had watched the man with the knife straddle the gator and begin to skin it. Then he heard Miss Lockey call for him from the big house.

The man skinning the gator heard her too and he looked up.

It was Jim Pitts. Younger. Darker hair. But still the same surly mouth and sullen eyes.

Forrest woke. He opened his eyes and found that gray-white fog had crawled up to the rear veranda.

Miss Lockey? Yes, he remembered her now. He had been in her charge when he was young. Miss Lockey was tall and thin and she had been firm and sternly affectionate. She had been with the family until Forrest had turned twelve and been sent off to the boarding school in New England.

Forrest's eyes closed. When he woke again, it was nearly eight o'clock in the morning. He dressed and took the rear stairs down to the back garden.

The fog had thinned, though here and there dense patches of it still persisted under the trees. In the wispy distance he could just make out a hill. Yes, Thompson's Hill.

But it wasn't really a hill, he remembered. The island had no real hills. They were just large ancient sand dunes covered with sparse vegetation and struggling trees.

Forrest smelled something burning. Something acrid, chemical.

He turned a hedge and found MacIntyre crouched on the path, his hands shielding a small flame from what breeze there might be. Whatever he was burning soon burned black and the flame died.

MacIntyre rose and ground his heel into the small pile of ash. He brushed his trouser knees and picked up his briefcase. When he turned and saw Forrest, he colored. "How long have you been there?"

"About twenty seconds."

MacIntyre licked his lips. "I was burning some notes concerning a paper I'm writing. I don't like to just toss them into the wastebasket when I'm through with them. Prying servants, you know, and I don't like people reading my things before they're published."

Forrest's attention was distracted by a movement on Thompson's Hill.

MacIntyre saw it too and squinted. "Someone's up there."

They watched the distant figure racing through the dissipating fog.

MacIntyre sighed. "I suppose that's Henry jogging again."

"No," Forrest said. "Whoever he is, he's not jogging. He's running like hell."

A large yellow and black striped animal bounded into view behind the fleeing man. It caught up with him in a matter of seconds and brought him down. The man's thin screams carried to them and then stopped.

"My God," MacIntyre whispered. "What was that?"

"A tiger," Forrest said softly. "A tiger."

"But that's impossible."

"It's not impossible. We're looking at it."

The huge beast raised its head from the body and stared in their direction.

MacIntyre's voice was barely audible. "Does it see us?"

"I don't know."

"How far away is it?"

"Half a mile. About that."

The tiger's jaws gripped the body by its neck and dragged it out of sight into the trees.

"My God," MacIntyre said again.

Forrest moved. "We'd better get back inside the

19

house."

"Yes," MacIntyre agreed quickly. "Back into the house." He trotted after Forrest.

Forrest went directly to Hegan's den. He removed the Weatherby from its brackets and pulled back the bolt. "Where does Hegan keep his ammunition?"

MacIntyre's eyes flitted about the room. "I really don't know."

"Start looking." Forrest opened a drawer of Hegan's desk and found a small carton. He shook it. "Here's what the cartridges come in, but this one's empty."

After ten minutes, Forrest gave up. "Nothing. At least not in this room. We'd better wake people and tell them that we have a tiger on our hands. One of them ought to know where we can find the ammunition. I suppose you know where Pitts and the Bowlers sleep? I'll wake the others."

MacIntyre hesitated. "The Bowlers have their own room next to the kitchen downstairs. But Pitts sleeps in one of the old slave cabins out back. Do you think it's safe to go out there?"

"I don't think there's any real danger right now. The tiger's probably busy chewing on what he's got."

Forrest met Henry at the top of the stairs on the second floor veranda.

Henry wore a sweat shirt and shorts. "I was just about to go jogging."

"I wouldn't recommend it this morning, Henry."

"I know. I saw what happened from up here. I've been watching the spot since then, but I haven't seen the tiger again."

"Do you know who the tiger killed?"

"Not really. It happened a little too far away for me to be certain."

"You'd better wake your mother and your sister and Miss Deveraux."

"Yes. I suppose so."

"Do you know where your father keeps the ammunition for his rifle?"

"Somewhere in the den, I think."

20

Forrest decided to give Hegan's den one more try. He was still searching when Oriana Deveraux appeared in the doorway.

Her face was pale. "Henry told me that there's a tiger on the island."

"Yes. It just killed someone on Thompson's Hill. I don't know how the hell the tiger got here, but it's here."

Laurie and Henry appeared in the doorway.

Laurie smiled skeptically. "How in the world could a tiger get to this island? I thought they lived in Asia."

"Tigers can swim," Henry said.

They looked at him.

He flushed slightly. "I don't mean that the tiger swam all the way from Asia. Or even from our mainland. Even that would be too far. Tigers can swim, and some even like to, but they just wouldn't have the stamina to cover anything like the distance from the mainland."

Henry blinked several times. "I mean this tiger could have been in a cage on the deck of a ship. And this ship got wrecked just off the shore, and the cage broke, and the tiger swam to the island."

"All right, Henry," Laurie said soothingly. "We'll say that it's just possible."

Eve joined them. "Where's Mike?"

"He went back to the mainland early this morning," Laurie said. "He told me he had business to take care of and he didn't want to be held up by the fog."

MacIntyre brought Bowler and Bowler's wife, Clara, into the room.

Bowler was a small, portly man, his face ruddy with indignation. "Mr. MacIntyre didn't tell us anything at all about there being a tiger out there until after he sent me to wake Pitts. I could have gotten killed and eaten."

Bowler's wife was several inches taller than her husband, with red-brown hair and a full figure. She frowned at all of them suspiciously.

"Where is Pitts?" Forrest asked.

"He wasn't there," Bowler snapped petulantly. "His place was empty. And dirty. He doesn't even use sheets on his bed."

Henry cleared his throat. "Actually I don't believe we're in too much danger for at least twenty-four hours. More likely forty-eight. What I mean is that the tiger will gorge himself and then probably go to sleep. And if there's anything left, he'll go back to the body a second day. Maybe a third."

Laurie counted heads. "Let's face it. Everybody's here or accounted for except Pitts."

Clara Bowler sank into a chair, her face pale.

"Does anyone know where there might be some ammunition for the rifle? I've already checked this room."

There were blank stares.

Forrest sighed. "In that case, I suggest that we barricade this house."

"That might not be so easy," Eve said. "There's really nothing much between us and the tiger except glass and screening, and in some places, not even that."

"Pitts has a double-barreled shotgun," Henry said. "And shells. They might still be in his cabin. I'll take a look."

Forrest followed him. "I think it might be better if you had company, Henry."

They paused on the rear veranda and then moved down the stairs to the back garden.

Henry led the way over a narrow beaten path until they reached a double row of tabby-plastered single-room cabins. Most of their roofs had long ago collapsed, but the walls still remained intact.

Henry stopped at one of the roofed cabins. The rusted-out screen door squeaked as he pulled it open. "This is where Pitts slept."

Murky light pushed through the dirt of a single small window. Forrest stepped into the room and picked up the double-barreled shotgun leaning against the corner of the room. "Twenty gauge. Not exactly made for tiger hunting."

"That's the only gun Pitts has," Henry said. "It came with the house."

Forrest rummaged through a cardboard box on the

small table next to Pitts' bunk. "The only shells he seems to have are No. 7 birdshot. That won't help us a bit."

Henry agreed. "No. 7 shot would only make a tiger angry, not kill him." He cocked his head and appeared to be listening. "It's suddenly gotten awful quiet out there. No birds and things."

Henry moved back to the door and smiled. "Our tiger's right outside."

Forrest quietly joined him at the door.

Henry pointed. "There he is. Straight ahead at the end of the land, lying in the high grass. You can see his tail twitching."

Forrest slipped two shells into the shotgun.

Henry shook his head. "I don't think it's a good idea to use that."

"I wasn't going to, Henry. It just makes me feel better holding a loaded gun."

They remained motionless, staring at the tiger. Long minutes passed.

At last the tiger rose and stretched. He moved forward a dozen feet and crouched again, his tail flicking back and forth.

Henry whispered. "I don't think he sees us or knows we're in here. At least he's not looking directly at us. And we're down wind."

Another minute passed and Henry spoke again. "Something has his attention. I think it's those yellow butterflies."

The tiger yawned elaborately and rose. He turned and loped away through the high grass and disappeared behind the row of cabins.

Forrest exhaled slowly and eased open the screen door. They hurried back to the house.

Inside, Forrest closed the French doors behind him. "Not even a lock on these damn things. Not that it would really make any difference, I suppose."

MacIntyre wiped his forehead. "Thank God you've got Pitts' shotgun."

"It won't stop a tiger," Henry said and smiled. "We saw the tiger again out there. Maybe he killed Pitts just for the sport of it. People think that predators kill only when they're hungry, but that isn't true."

They waited.

"The tiger was lean at the belly," Henry said. "Not gorged at all. So it looks like he didn't eat Pitts, or at least not more than a bite or two. Maybe it was the alcohol."

Laurie sighed. "What alcohol, Henry?"

"In Pitts. He was almost always under the influence of alcohol. It was in his stomach and in his blood, you know, and animals don't like alcohol. Maybe rats in laboratories do, once they're trained to it, but not animals in the wild. So it could be that the tiger tasted Pitts and just couldn't stand the alcohol.

"Is there any way we can communicate with the mainland?" Forrest asked.

Laurie shook her head. "I'm afraid not. And Mike took the only boat we have, so we can't get off the island until he gets back. That should be sometime this afternoon."

Henry had an idea. "Why don't we all get into the station wagon and drive down to the wharf and wait for Mike? I've seen pictures of people in cars in Africa. They stop and let lions crawl all over and they're perfectly safe just as long as they stay inside their cars."

"That's the first thing I thought of," NacIntyre said testily, "but the station wagon is gone. I'll bet Pitts took it and it's somewhere near where the tiger got him."

Henry nodded eagerly. "I'll go out and look for it."

Laurie stopped him. "Like hell you will. You stay right here."

"That leaves us with a problem," Eve said. "Without the station wagon we have to remain here. But that means that when Mike comes back, he runs the risk of getting killed by the tiger while walking up to the house."

"We could leave a note on one of the pilings," Henry said, "warning him about the tigers."

Laurie went to the typewriter and rolled in a sheet of paper. She used two fingers to type.

> *Dear Mike:*
> *There's a real live tiger loose*

on this island. Or at least every-
body tells me there is. I haven't
seen it yet. We don't know how
it got here, but they say it killed
Pitts. I didn't see that either.
Don't try to walk up to the
house. Go back to the mainland
for help. We have your rifle, but
there's no ammunition.

   Love, Laurie

Henry had been reading over her shoulder. "That ought to do it. I'll take it out and tack it somewhere where he'll see it first thing. I'll get a pan from the kitchen."

He looked at their blank faces. "You know, like the beaters in India. They have hordes of them at the tiger hunts. They're totally unarmed, except for those pans and they beat them and drive the tiger toward the hunter. I'll take along a pan and if I meet the tiger, I'll bang it and drive hime away."

"Henry," Laurie said, "if you so much as see the tiger, I want you to climb a tree."

Henry smiled. "Tigers can climb trees."

MacIntyre scowled. "You seem to know an awful lot about tigers."

Henry agreed. "I looked them up once in an encyclopedia and somehow I remembered everything."

Henry went downstairs to the kitchen and returned with a tin dishpan and a wooden spoon. He folded the note and pocketed it along with a box of thumb tacks.

They watched him from the railing of the front veranda.

Henry walked jauntily down the driveway. He looked back, waved, then broke into a trot.

"He's crazy," MacIntyre said. "Crazy."

four

The Bowlers returned to their kitchen and the others went upstairs, but Oriana lingered.

She watched Forrest going through the drawers of the desk once more. She smiled faintly. "Whatever happened to the pony?"

Forrest looked up. "Pony?"

"Yes, the little black and white pony."

"Bobby? I really don't remember. I suppose he was sold or maybe he just died of old age. How did you know I had a pony?"

"I saw him once when I was a very little girl. I woke one morning and there he was, chewing on what was left of our flower garden. I wanted to believe that he was a present but my mother told me that he didn't belong to us. He had just wandered off from the Forrest plantation. I went out and petted him and talked to him. In the afternoon Pitts came and took him away."

"Pitts?"

"Yes. He was one of the caretakers at the Forrest plantation after you and your parents left. Ben Williams and his wife, Odie, took care of the house and Pitts was responsible for the grounds. When Ben died, Odie moved in with relatives on the mainland and that left only my mother and me on the island. Except for Pitts."

Oriana was silent for a moment. "And soon after that the Forrest plantation house burned to the ground. I saw the lightning strike and then the sky lit up with fire. I was right here on the second floor veranda when it happened. There was nothing anyone could do, really. So I just watched. And then Pitts left the island too."

Forrest had stopped searching for cartridges and was watching her pale face. "And that left Deveraux the only great house still standing on the island?"

"Yes, the only one still standing."

Oriana remembered the rooms empty of furniture and the broken windows. There had been dust and decay and peeling wallpaper.

She and her mother had occupied two rooms downstairs--the kitchen and the small bedroom adjoining it. Oriana had slept on a cot in the kitchen.

And Oriana remembered the silence. Her mother had almost never spoken to her.

It had been necessary for them to plant a vegetable garden so that they could survive and she remembered her mother slashing savagely at the weeds with her hoe, her eyes burning with hatred at what she had to do.

And then one day, when Oriana was still quite small, she had said, "I'll take care of the garden, Mother. You go back to the house and the shade."

Her mother had glared at her. "Why?"

"Because you hate it so much."

Her mother had taken off her gardening gloves and dropped them on the ground. She had walked away and never set foot in the vegetable garden again.

Her mother had always slept until ten in the morning. When she rose, her eyes would go to the clock again and again during the day waiting for five o'clock.

At five, she would get into her nightgown and fetch one of the brandy bottles from the wooden cases in the cellar. She would sit at the kitchen table, slowly sipping brandy from a water glass and playing game after game of solitaire.

At eight o'clock, she would put the deck aside, carefully make her way to the bedroom and go to sleep.

Then one morning when Oriana woke, she had looked into the bedroom and seen that her mother was dead.

Oriana had waited at the wharf for the mail boat and told the pilot what had happened. He had returned to the island in the afternoon with two men to dig the grave and a minister to say the services. When the boat left, Oriana had been aboard with one suitcase. She had been nearly eighteen years old.

Oriana's mind was brought back to the present by the distand sound of metal being beaten frantically.

"Damn," Forrest said. "It's Henry."

He picked up the shotgun and stepped outside.

The beating stopped.

"Stay inside," he ordered Oriana. He raced down the stairs and onto the driveway, but at the first bend in the road, he slowed, moving more cautiously.

He had nearly reached the wharf when he found Henry seated on a fallen tree, the dishpan on his lap.

Forrest closed the distance. "Where's the tiger, Henry?"

Henry smiled. "He ran down to the beach."

"Banging on that dishpan scared him off?"

"Yes." Henry tapped the dishpan absently several times with the wooden spoon and then got to his feet. "I guess we might just as well go back to the house."

"Did you leave the note at the dock?"

Henry blinked. "The note? Oh, yes. But I don't think that it really matters. Mike probably won't be coming back today. The ocean's beginning to swell and you can see in the sky that there's a storm coming up. If it gets bad, a small boat would be taking a big chance trying to cross over from the mainland. And Mike wouldn't take that kind of a chance in a storm. Not when it comes to water. He can't swim, you know." Henry looked up at the sky. "It's going to rain soon. Rain and wind. Maybe even a hurricane. The note I left on the wharf will get all wet and blow away. But when the storm's over I'll go back and tack up another one. In the morning, maybe."

They had almost reached the house when Henry sighed. "I might as well tell you the truth."

"Truth about what, Henry?"

"There wasn't any tiger. At least I didn't see any."

"You just decided to beat that pan to see what it sounded like?"

Henry nodded. "That and I wanted to see who might come to find out what happened to me. You don't suppose they'll be disappointed? I mean, here they expect me to eaten by a tiger and I turn up safe and sound."

"Not disappointed, Henry. But possibly a little irritated if you tell them the truth."

When they entered the house, Laurie, Oriana and Eve were waiting.

Laurie touched Henry lightly on the shoulder. "Are you all right, Henry?"

Forrest spoke for him. "Yes, he's all right. He chased the tiger away."

It began to rain.

five

Bowler squinted in the effort to see through the rain-blurred kitchen windows. He could make out nothing.

Coming down in buckets. Buckets.

And that's good. Cats don't like wet weather and what is a tiger but a big cat. That damn animal won't be roaming around out there, now or tonight, if the rain keeps up. He'll be holed up somewhere where it's dry.

Bowler poured himself a cup of tea and added a little brandy. He would wait until eleven o'clock tonight. When everybody was asleep. Or at least up in their bedrooms.

The windows rattled with a sudden gust. Bowler swung toward them, half expecting to see the face of the tiger. But there was nothing. Nothing but rain.

Bowler's eyes lingered for a moment on Clara's apron hanging on a wall peg. Damn fool woman.

As far as looks went, Clara wasn't really too bad. But when you finally noticed those eyes--really paid attention to them--you could see what was there. She was a domineering woman. Yes, definitely domineering.

Bowler had seen that in her eyes from the very beginning and he would have had absolutely nothing whatever to do with her, if it hadn't been for that damn bankbook.

He had been in Hegan's employ for three weeks before he had found the opportunity to go through Clara's room. She had left for a movie and he had made certain that she was really gone before he let himself into her room.

Everything had been neat, tidy, predictable. The bed, the dresser, the severe chair, exactly and unimaginatively placed. He had sniffed the perfume vial on her dresser.

Utterly without character.

What had he been looking for? Nothing in particular, but you could never tell what might turn up.

He had opened one of the bureau drawers. Some loose change in a glass jar had caught his attention. He had counted the money. Ninety-eight cents. He had put two dimes and a nickle into his pocket and returned the rest of the coins to the jar.

He had lightly touched the stack of handkerchiefs.

Something under there.

He had pulled out the little green bankbook and smiled. Ah, what do we have here?

He had opened the book and raised an eyebrow. Over ten thousand dollars. Well, well.

He had stood there thinking about that. Yes, it figured. As far as he had been able to observe so far, Clara almost never went anywhere, never spent any money.

How old was she? Middle thirties? Probably been working since she left high school. And saving money.

Ten thousand dollars? And that was just the savings account. Was there more? Stocks? Bonds? All of them in safe stocks and bonds. No speculation, if he read Clara correctly.

He had smiled as he carefully replaced the bankbook under the handkerchiefs. He had paused a moment and then regretfully returned the two dimes and the nickle to the glass jar. One must not jeopardize the larger venture for a few piddling coins. Clara might notice they were missing and begin to wonder.

Now Bowler sipped his tea and stared moodily at his distorted image on the side of the polished teakettle. Baldness runs in my family, he thought. My father. My grandfather--from what little I remember of him.

Bowler's father had been a butler and so had his grandfather. All of the male Bowlers had been butlers almost since the dawn of time, it seemed. They had always lived in other people's big houses.

But Bowler himself had always had rather bad luck with employers. Really, some of them had even threatened to turn him over to the police. Rich men they were, too, and what possible difference could a few loose dollars here and there have really meant to them?

It was fortunate that he had always kept his eyes open and usually he had been in a position to create some degree of trouble if he were pressed too far. And so he had always managed to get excellent letters of recommendation when he had been forced to leave.

He sighed heavily. But what am I now? A butler? Most of the time I'm really a chauffeur, a dog-walker, a handyman, a what-have-you for the occasion. And as far as Clara was concerned, also the assistant cook.

Courting and claiming Clara had been childishly simple. The woman appeared never to have had any male attention in her entire life.

In a matter of four weeks they had been married in a brief civil ceremony and had gone to Niagara Falls--of all places--for their three day honeymoon.

Bowler had waited another two weeks before he had brought up the subject of money. "Dear," he had said over breakfast, "marriage is a fifty-fifty proposition, don't you agree?"

As he remembered, she had nodded cautiously.

He had put down his cup. "I've been thinking that we really ought to open a joint savings account. Pool our money, you know. I mean my money is yours and all that."

She had smiled. "Whatever you think is best, Andrew."

There had been a bit of a silence before Bowler had continued. "We'll go down to the bank at the first opportunity and open the joint account. Where do you bank?"

She had buttered her toast. "Bank? But I don't have a savings account, Andrew. None at all."

He had felt a slight chill. "You don't have a savings account?"

"No."

Bowler had managed a smile. "Of course it's your own business, I suppose, but you seem thrifty and all that and I just thought that you might have put something aside for a rainy day."

She had remained all innocence. "I'm afraid that I've

saved nothing at all. It's my brother. In Canada. He has a large family and he's had his troubles, and so I've been sending him every spare cent I have."

He had stared at her. Did she really expect him to believe a story like that?

The black eyes had turned once more upon him. "But you're right about the joint account, Andrew. I'll send a letter to my brother and tell him that I can't send him any more money. His children are now really old enough to help him financially. And also--starting with this month's paycheck--we'll put our money into a joint account. And save every cent we can. Isn't that right, Andrew?"

So that was the way it was going to be? She wasn't going to let him get his hands on any of her money? Should he tell her that he knew that she had at least ten thousand dollars in the bank? He had met those black eyes for a moment. No. That wouldn't be the right tactic at all. Not at all.

He had manufactured a smile. "That was awfully nice of you, Clara. Helping your brother and his family all those years."

Bowler had waited three weeks before he had tried again. After their supper in the kitchen, he had sighed pointedly.

"What's wrong?" A sharpness had been appearing in Clara's voice lately.

He had shrugged slightly. "I don't think there's anything you could do about it."

"Try me."

He had wilted slightly under her scrutiny, but had managed to speak up. "I thought they'd never find me, but they did. Two of them came to see me yesterday and they put it on the line. Huge fellows."

"What are you talking about?"

"Before we married...long before I met you...I used to bet quite heavily on the horses. With this bookie. And I lost, of course. It's always working out that way, it seems. And the upshot of the whole mess is that I still owe them ten thousand dollars and they want it very badly."

"Still owe?"

"Yes. Ten thousand." He had wet his lips. "The point is that they refuse to wait any longer. They're demanding that I pay everything I owe immediately or they will take drastic action."

"Who is they?"

"The Syndicate."

"What Syndicate?"

He had fumed impatiently. "**The** Syndicate. They demand immediate payment and if I don't come up with the money in twenty-four hours...." He had stopped. "Well, you know how those Syndicate people work."

"No," she had said. "I don't."

He had found himself flushing. "People just don't welsh on gambling debts to the Syndicate. They just don't."

"Gambling debts are uncollectable in this state. If they're threatening you, go to the police."

His voice had risen. "You can't do that. It wouldn't do any good. They get to you anyway. Nobody bucks the Syndicate. I need the ten thousand."

She had formed a final smile. "I really don't know what we can do about it anyway. We just don't have ten thousand dollars, do we?"

He had exploded. "We don't have ten thousand dollars! But you do!"

Her voice had been a purr. "Really? Now how would you know that?"

Bowler had pulled himself together and even tried a smile. "I accidently came across your bankbook while I was searching for some cuff links."

She had laughed, just slightly. "Now suppose that I really do have a bank account. Do you think that I'm the kind of person who would carelessly leave her deposit book lying in a bureau drawer?"

"But it was there," Bowler had insisted. "Beneath the handkerchiefs." For one wild moment he had sincerely regretted having returned the two dimes and the nickle to the glass jar.

Clara had become slyly thoughtful. "Now that I come

34

to think of it, I did once leave my bankbook under a pile of handkerchiefs. But that was before we were married. I remember I went to a movie that night. It was quite a good picture, too."

Bowler's eyes had widened. Now he saw it all. She had deliberately left the bankbook for him to find. She had known that he would go through her things. It had all been a trap! The whole blasted thing. The only possible way she could get him was to...

Damn the woman. Damn, damn, damn her.

He had almost burst into tears as he had stormed out of the room.

But then once again he had faced the situation. True, he had been duped into the marriage, but the fact still remained that Clara did have ten thousand dollars. And possibly more.

He had forced himself to think rationally. Yes, he had been trapped into the marriage, but didn't that at least indicate that she had wanted him enough to set the trap? Was that possible affection a lever which he could use?

Or had she just wanted a man? Any man? Had she reached her middle thirties and become panic-stricken at the thought of spinsterhood?

He had sighed. This was all going to be considerably more difficult than he had imagined. It would take time. Plenty of time. And he would have to be clever. Nothing as clumsy as the Syndicate play again. Should he go back to the kitchen smiling? No. That would be too obvious, too transparent. Too soon.

No, he had decided, he would play it as a normal indignant husband. He would not talk to Clara for two or three days. And even after that he would continue to show resentment for a time. That would be normal. Expected.

And then a gradual melting? He would pay more attention to Clara. Little things. Flowers. Candy. The whole damn bit.

That had been his plan. His campaign.

But then this blasted island and Jim Pitts came into the picture.

Bowler hadn't liked the island at all. Much too isolated. More than half of the time he and Clara and Pitts were the only persons on the island.

Pitts.

The man was quite impossible. Hulking and brutish and that terrible temper. It was apparent that his life had been one long dissipation. Drink had left its mark on his face and he wasn't at all careful about his person either. Unshaven most of the time and Bowler doubted whether Pitts was very familiar with a bathtub or a shower.

Really, Bowler couldn't understand at all just what Clara saw in that man.

Of course it had been perfectly obvious from the very beginning. The mutual...the peasant...attraction they had had for each other.

It wasn't that Bowler was jealous. Good Heavens, not that. He was even...well...relieved. Clara could be a bit demanding in some gross areas.

No, it had been the principle of the thing which had disturbed him. That, and, of course, the money.

After all, he was her husband and if she was going to give away any of her money, surely it should be to her own husband.

But she had actually begun giving money to Pitts.

Bowler had seen one of the transactions from a second story window. His binoculars hadn't been quite powerful enough to make out the denominations of the bills she had handed Pitts, but it had been money. He was certain of that.

So was that why Pitts always seemed to have money enough for his liquor?

Bowler had watched Clara give Pitts the money and then the two of them had embraced, if one could use that word for something they did so earthily. And if Pitts hadn't had to go to the mainland, Bowler felt that perhaps right there and then, in the back garden, they might have...

Bowler had shivered and experienced the indignant impulse to rush right down there and confront the two of them, but he had hesitated. There was no telling what an animal like Pitts might do. He might possibly turn violent.

Bowler had waited until Pitts was gone before he had hurried downstairs. He had found Clara in the kitchen and he had come directly to the point. "I saw you giving Pitts money. Do you deny it?"

She had fixed him with the black eyes. "Have you been spying on me?"

He had flushed. "Of course not. It was just an accident. I happened to be looking out of the window." He had tried to resume the offensive. "How much did you give him? And why?"

"Twenty dollars."

He had sputtered. "You gave him twenty dollars?"

She had smiled. "I've been giving him money for some time now."

Bowler's eyes had widened. She had come right out with it. She hadn't even tried to conceal the whole sordid affair. "But why, Clara. Why?"

She had laughed.

But that was all over with now.

Bowler's eyes went to the clock. He would wait until eleven tonight. He put more brandy into his cup and raised it in a toast.

To the tiger.

six

Bowler had informed her that MacIntyre would not be down for meals.

Poor Jamie, Laurie thought.

He had those watery eyes even when he was a kid, and that mousey-brown hair that was so thin and always blowing in all directions, and he always ran scared.

She and Jamie were cousins. Second or third, or something. Laurie had never been able to sort it out exactly. Probably they weren't even that close because they were such different types.

Jamie's father had been the neighborhood undertaker. Nowadays they call them funeral directors or morticians, or whatever, but in those days they were undertakers and the MacIntyre Funeral Home was in the middle of the block--not like funeral homes today which are always on a corner lot and have plenty of grass all around. MacIntyre's wasn't too big a building either. Two stories high and brick, but not very wide.

It was built right up to the sidewalk, with two No Parking signs in front and whenever anybody opened the front door, you could hear the recorded organ music inside.

The MacIntyres lived upstairs on the second floor. Mr. MacIntyre and Jamie and Jamie's mother. There was a back outside entrance so that you didn't have to go through the first floor and disturb anything happening when you came to visit.

The first floor was where they had the viewing room

with the casket stand and the folding chairs, and Mr. MacIntyre's private office, and also a private grieving alcove behind heavy purple drapes for the immediate family if they wanted to use it. And in the basement Mr. MacIntyre did the work on the bodies and sometimes he'd have two or three down there at once, at least according to Jamie.

Laurie had never been down there and she had never wanted to go, even though Jamie had offered her the chance to see a corpse when his father wasn't there.

All the kids in the neighborhood used to watch the MacIntyre chimneys and when they saw smoke coming out they knew that Mr. MacIntyre was burning parts of a body, like the insides. Jamie said it was to make the body as light as possible so that the pall bearers' wouldn't complain about the weight. Even to this day, she still didn't know if Jamie was kidding or not, because he wasn't much of a kidder.

There was a tailor shop on one side of the MacIntyre Funeral Home and a tavern on the other. Herman and Bessie's Tap. In the warm summer evenings when the tavern door was propped open for ventilation, she would pass by and she would usually see Mr. MacIntyre at the bar.

People said he spent most of his time in there, but the liquor and the beer didn't really show. He didn't stagger or anything. Sometimes he smelt a little of beer, but mostly it was Listerine. Mr. MacIntyre always wore a business suit and a white carnation in his lapel.

Everybody called him Mister MacIntyre. Not Mac or just MacIntyre, but Mister MacIntyre. Probably because wearing a business suit on weekdays in that neighborhood made you stand out.

Mrs. MacIntyre hardly ever left the second floor apartment to go anywhere. She was a tall woman with dark eyes who always looked like she had a headache.

Laurie and her mother would go up there by the back stairs to visit about two or three times a year, because after all they were relatives, and they usually stayed for one hour, but it seemed a lot longer.

Mrs. MacIntyre had all of those religious pamphlets

and all she ever talked about was Judgment Day. She was always positive it was going to happen every year and she would give you the exact day and time.

When Laurie and her mother got home, Laurie would tell her father about the Judgment Day prediction for this year and he would put a circle around the date on the calendar. The day would come with no judgment and Dad would shake his head and say, "Damn it, and here I was ready to go."

Her father worked at the Garrison Outboard Motor company. The hours and the pay were good because they had a strong union and everybody stuck together when they had to.

Her father was a big, good-looking man. Not fat. Just maybe ten or fifteen pounds overweight and he had real nice blue eyes and straw-colored hair. In the summer he played league softball for the Jacobi Furniture team and in the winter he was in two bowling leagues, Tuesday and Friday nights. His average was somewhere around one hundred eighty-five, which was pretty good, and he had a dozen or so team trophies which were kept on the mantel of the imitation fireplace.

Her father died when Laurie was seventeen. A heart attack everybody guessed, because it happened in his sleep and he was just dead the next morning.

Dad's funeral was probably the biggest and best that Mr. MacIntyre had ever handled. Laurie hadn't known that her father was that important and popular, but there was a terrific turnout and even a traffic jam in front of MacIntyre's when it came time for the procession to the cemetery. It took three or four cops to finally get everything moving.

Dad's softball team and their wives and kids showed up and the bowling teams and a whole crowd from the outboard motor factory. At the grave side, there was even a firing squad from the American Legion post.

Everybody had a good cry and felt a lot better and then they all came back to the house where there were two quarter-barrels of beer set up in the back yard. There was ham, cold cuts, bratwursts, salads and casseroles, and all kins of pies, cakes and brownies brought by the mourners and the neighbors. The last of the people didn't leave until after eleven that night and the grass back there was just about killed for the summer.

Laurie had good parents and really good homelife, for which she was thankful. She didn't remember her mother or her father particularly arguing about anything serious and the family was just the right size. She had three brothers and one sister and they got along just fine usually, except for a few spats, which you have to expect.

But Jamie had no family really. Just him and his mother reading those pamphlets and telling him that the world was going to end before he had a chance to grow up.

Poor Jamie. She still thought of him that way, even though today he was doctor and all. Somehow you just felt that he never did get to pull all the pieces together.

Not like Mike.

Mike always knew what he was doing.

They had met in high school when she was a freshman. Mike never had any trouble getting girls and he must have known plenty, but he seemed to settle down when they started going together.

It had all come so natural. She hadn't felt guilty or thought she was going to hell or anything silly like that. It was just something that you did sooner or later when you like somebody, but just the same you didn't let your parents know what was going on, even though things like that happened through the ages and probably to your parents too.

There had been this old garage behind Mike's father's house. It was a wooden building that had once been a barn. There was room downstairs for two cars and upstairs there was a loft where people had kept hay for their horses in the old days.

Mike and she would sneak up there after school and use the mattress and pillows that he'd smuggled up there.

In the summertime it sometimes got too warm up there, so Mike would open a trap door at one end of the barn and try to get a little cool breeze.

She hadn't been worried that anybody would see them through that opening because there was a tree just outside the building and it was like a curtain of green leaves.

But one afternoon when she and Mike had finished and were just lying there thinking, she had looked up and seen Jamie's face in among the leaves.

He had shinnied up there and been bug-eyed watching what they were doing.

She had almost screamed, but then she had suddenly thought, My God, if Mike sees Jamie in that tree he'll kill him for sure. So she had said nothing, but when Mike had his back to her, she had pointed a finger right up at Jamie and her lips had silently moved to say, "Damn it, go!"

Jamie's face had disappeared back into the leaves and she could just make out the sound when he jumped back to the ground, but luckily Mike hadn't heard it.

She had been worried sick that Jamie might tell somebody what he had seen and so when she got home she phoned the private number the MacIntyres had for their apartment and asked to talk to Jamie. Mrs. MacIntyre had said that Jamie wasn't home yet, but she expected him for supper.

So Laurie had hurried over to the funeral home and hid beside the back stairs and waited.

It had been nearly five-thirty when Jamie had showed up and opened the back gate. When he saw her, he had ducked into the side door of the garage where Mr. MacIntyre kept his hearse and the big black Cadillac passenger car.

Laurie had run up to the garage door and opened it. "Jamie, I want to talk to you. Right now. This minute."

But there had been just quietness and she hadn't seen Jamie anywhere inside. But she knew he had to be in there because there was no other way out except through the big garage doors and they were shut.

So she had searched the garage until she had found Jamie in the back of the passenger Cadillac trying to hide on the floor.

She had pulled open the back door and said, "Well, what do you have to say for yourself, Peeping Tom?"

Jamie's face had been white and he had said nothing.

"I suppose now that you're going to tell everybody? The whole neighborhood?"

42

He had shook his head no.

"How did you know we were up there?" she had said, really glaring at him.

He couldn't look her in the eyes and he had finally said, "I followed you two sometimes and I saw you go into the garage."

She had blinked. "And just how many times were you up in that tree watching?"

"A few times. Not so many."

He had looked so scared that she had gotten a little soft hearted. "You're not going to tell anybody, are you?"

"No," he had said real earnestly. "I won't. I swear it, Laurie. I would never do anything like that."

Then he had looked at her real funny.

And she had seen in his eyes what he wanted and it had shocked her. Really shocked her, because you just somehow didn't expect anything like that coming from Jamie. Not Jamie.

But he had looked so lonely. So lost and helpless, really, that she had felt sorry for him.

So she had gotten into the back of the Cadillac and shut the door behind her and helped him unbutton his shirt and things.

When they had finished undressing, they had lain there and she had felt Jamie trembling all over.

Poor Jamie. She had been patient and understanding, but he just couldn't do anything. After about half an hour, she had told him that it was supper time and she had to go home and she thought that he was really relieved.

After they dressed, she had watched him leave the garage for the house and he didn't look back.

She had never told Mike anything about Jamie. She and Mike still used the loft, of course, but she would always make sure that Jamie wasn't in the tree first and he never was again.

Laurie had been worried about other things too in those days because there wasn't any such thing as the pill and Mike wouldn't use anything. He always said that if you couldn't go in barefoot, it wasn't worth doing at all.

At least a dozen girls in her class had had to leave high school before they graduated and Laurie had thought for sure that that would happen to her too, but it didn't.

In Mike's senior year, he had sort of changed. Not that anything got cold between them--that was always good--but he would get vague and stare into space when she talked about them marrying after he got his diploma.

Finally he had told her that he'd been thinking things over and he had decided to go on to college.

That had really floored her because Mike wasn't the kind of person who went in for books or any more education than he had to. And now that she thought about it, she couldn't offhand remember anybody else from the neighborhood going on to college, except Jamie.

She had figured that Mike would go to the university downtown because that way he could still live at home and get free room and board, but Mike decided to go to a small college down south that had less than five hundred students. Mike said that it was a place where a lot of rich people sent their kids after they flunked out of other places, but their parents still wanted them to get a degree of some kind or not be underfoot.

She had asked him what he was going to study down there--like medicine or law or denistry--and he said that it was going to be tennis. She couldn't quite decide whether he was fooling or not, because he did get himself a racket and he would go to the tennis courts in Washington Park and practice for hours against the backboards.

She had also asked him how he could afford to go to a rich people's college and he had said never mind, I'll swing it some way.

When he did go down there, he wasn't much of a letter writer. Just a short note now and then. And then out-of-the-blue, at the end of the first semester, he wrote that he'd met this girl, Myra, and decided to marry her.

Just like that. Out-of-the-blue. No advance notice or anything.

Of course Laurie had been stunned. But that's life. You have to take the bad with the good and so she had just squared her shoulders and gone on.

44

Laurie never actually got to meet Myra in the flesh, but she had seen snapshots. Myra was small and dark and wasn't at all good looking and Laurie couldn't figure why Mike married her. But then Henry was born five months after the ceremony and that must have been the reason.

Now Laurie went to the French windows and looked out at the rain.

She sighed. You just never did know what Fate had in store for you, now did you?

seven

MacIntyre locked the door.

This was probably the safest place in the house, he reassured himself. He would just have to wait here until Mike came back to the island and did something about the tiger.

He sat down. Thank God he still had the negatives in his safety deposit box. He could always make more copies.

He sighed. How things had changed since he was a kid. Nowadays you could go downtown in almost any good-sized city and pick up anything you wanted and it was out in the open.

But when he'd been twelve, things had been a lot tighter. He'd had to keep his eyes and his ears open and put a few things together before he found out how it all worked.

He'd gone to the magazine stand on the corner of Twelfth and Brady and bought half a dozen pulp magazines--things like Adventure Stories, Sports Stories, World War I Aces and even Love Stories. He'd taken them home up to the attic where he turned to the back pages of advertisements. He had begun sending out post cards and filling out application blanks for more information about things like how would you like to be an artist and draw real live models, and body building courses, and pictures of exotic beauties.

Of course he didn't care anything at all about being an artist or building up his body and he knew that the pictures of the exotic beauties weren't going to show anything but their faces, but that wasn't the point. The point was that after a while his name would get on certain private mailing lists.

MacIntyre had had to do a lot of planning. Like how could he get this stuff through the mail without his mother knowing. She was the kind of a person who would open your mail and had absolutely no respect for a person's private property.

But he'd heard about post office box numbers and he had gone downtown and discovered that they were cheap to rent. So once a week, and later twice and even three times, he would go downtown and pick up his mail.

He threw away most of the stuff he got at first and he didn't subscribe to any of the courses. He just patiently sent out more cards. After about two months, he began getting things in the mail that said his name had been recommended to them because he was an adult and had adult entertainment tastes and values. And maybe he would be interested in something that was very adult.

He'd been cheated a few times at first. Like the offer of six photos, 8 x 10. See the Tango as it's really done below the border, if you know what we mean. Something the tourists don't see. Exceptional poses. In plain wrapper.

$8.00.

When the package came, he'd rushed up to the attic and opened it. There had been just this same couple dancing in each picture. Even their clothes looked old fashioned. So he had torn up the pictures and charged it all up to experience.

But after a while, he began getting the real stuff. He'd been surprised at how much mail eventually came. He discovered all kinds of things that he'd never even dreamed of before. Like clubs that exchanged dirty clothes back and forth. But what really gave MacIntyre the icky feeling was the mail that must have come from the body building courses mailing lists. The last thing in the world he wanted to do was become a queer or look at that type of picture. Nowadays people had different attitudes, but in those days it was rotten and MacIntyre still felt the same way about it.

MacIntyre filled a paper cup with water and drank it.

Damn it. Maybe he shouldn't have burned those pictures after all. But on the other hand, while he was on this island, he couldn't just carry that briefcase with him wherever he went. People would ask why. And he certainly couldn't leave it in his bedroom anymore. Not with Bowler prowling around about and prying into things.

Had Bowler ever gotten into the briefcase? Did he really have a ring of keys that could open any lock? Or was Hegan just needling him again?

Damn Hegan. But at least MacIntyre was still one up on Hegan and always would be.

He'd watched Laurie and Hegan from that tree at least a dozen times. After school, he would see them walk off together. He knew where they were going and what they were going to do.

At first he'd just followed them and made sure that they didn't see him. They'd disappear into the old barn that was now a garage. And MacIntyre would wait outside and time them and imagine them doing all sorts of things.

Then one hot afternoon, he'd seen Hegan swing open a little trap door on the end of the barn. They'd probably wanted to get a little fresh air in there. And MacIntyre had seen that if someone climbed the big tree next to the barn, he could see what was really happening in there. He'd been tempted to shinny up right then and there, but he'd been afraid that they might hear him.

But the next day he was up there before they even got to the barn. When Hegan pushed open that trap door again, MacIntyre had had a good view of everything that happened.

He had watched them from the tree a dozen times and then one afternoon Laurie happened to look up and right at him and her eyes had gotten wide and angry. Her lips had moved and MacIntyre had been able to read, "Damn it, go!"

He had been in a panic when he slid down the tree and started running. What would Hegan do to him? Beat him up? Maybe even kill him?

48

But then MacIntyre had realized that Laurie's lips had just formed the words, "Damn it, go!" but there hadn't been any sound. Just her lips moving and giving the message.

That must mean that she didn't want Hegan to know that MacIntyre had been watching. Maybe she was scared of what Hegan might do if he found out.

But still MacIntyre had worried. Laurie might not tell Hegan that he had been spying, but what would she do about it herself? Yell at him or even hit him?

He had done a lot of walking until he saw that it was time to get home for supper and he couldn't be late. Once he had been half an hour late and his mother had called the police and reported him kidnapped.

When he had showed up she had shrieked at him and grabbed him by the arm and led him to the table where she kept her pamphlets. She had made him read a whole stack of them that had to do with your duty to your parents, especially your mother.

When MacIntyre had come up the alley to his house and into the yard, Laurie had jumped out of the shadows and almost scared him to death.

He had run into the garage and hidden in the back of the Cadillac. But she had come in after and found him.

He hadn't been ready for what happened next. Or what didn't happen.

MacIntyre felt a cold sweat about that now and tried to concentrate on something else.

In a way, being the son of an undertaker had some advantages. A lot of kids were afraid of you, especially when you told them that you touched a corpse every morning for luck and didn't wash your hands after. You could get them wide-eyed by telling them all kinds of stories about what went on in the basement.

And you knew that your father probably earned more money than anybody in the neighborhood. You always had good clothes and a generous allowance.

MacIntyre had thought that he was going to be an undertaker too. Like his father, only move to a better neighborhood and earn more money. He had really loved being down there in the basement watching his father and Mr.

Edmonds, his father's assistant, at work.

But his mother had been against it. She didn't want any son of hers to be an undertaker. Being married to one was bad enough and you couldn't really have any friends except the wives of other undertakers and she didn't know any.

His mother had a long talk with him and she had told him that he was going to be a doctor. She had made him swear on the Bible that that was what he wanted.

When she had finally let him go, he had gone down to the basement.

His father had looked up. "Is your mother finished telling you that you're going to be a doctor?"

"Yes, sir."

"You got any objections?"

MacIntyre had cleared his throat. "I thought it might be nice to become a mortician."

His father had reached for the can of beer on the marble slab. "There's nothing wrong with being an undertaker. It's a nice healthy profession and you don't break your back. And nobody ever heard of an undertaker going to a psychiatrist. But for once in her damn life, your mother might be right. You earn a lot more money being a doctor and you don't have to grin every time people ask you what you do for a living."

Every day after supper, his mother would clear the dining room table and make him do his homework. When he didn't have any assignments, she made him review and review.

Once when he'd had a headache, he'd asked her what was the use of studying so hard to be a doctor when the world was going to end this year on the twenty-eighth of July. She had slapped him and told him that she wasn't taking any sass.

It had been a long, rough and really boring time in medical school and MacIntyre had thought about dropping out. He had even mentioned that once to his mother. But she had screeched at him and called him an ungrateful son-of-a-bitch and so he hadn't brought up the subject again.

When he finished his internship, his mother had set

50

him up by buying old Dr. Walter's practice. Dr. Walters had his offices over the drugstore on the corner of Twelfth and Brady, where you could look down at the magazine stand.

It had been only two blocks from home and MacIntyre's mother had come over to the office every day. She talked to the patients and checked his books and she made him open a bank account which he wasn't supposed to touch until he had enough money to set up a practice in the suburbs and she would go with him. But she had died suddenly of a stroke three months after he took over Dr. Walters' practice.

MacIntyre's father could have handled the funeral. There was no law against it. But you just don't bury your own. So he had turned the whole thing over to Costigan, who was located on Thirty-seventh Street.

MacIntyre hadn't expected much of a turnout for the services, but he had been surprised. The minister from The Church of the Redeemed Souls had come with about two dozen of his flock-almost all of them women and somehow they had reminded him of his mother, just by the way their faces were set.

They had done a lot of loud praying, and crying, and wailing. MacIntyre had watched and then he had been startled to find himself giggling. It had been terribly embarassing, even though everybody thought that he was just expressing his grief by being hysterical.

When MacIntyre and his father had gotten home, his father had opened a bottle. "Do you drink? I don't remember if I ever asked."

"No, sir."

His father had poured a stiff drink for himself. His eyes had gone to the table piled with Bible tracts. "Those have got to go."

MacIntyre had found himself nodding agreement and then saying, "I think I'll have that drink after all."

His father had poured whiskey into a glass and handed it to him.

MacIntyre had thought about downing it straight, but then he had decided that he'd better not try to show off.

So he had added soda. The drink hadn't tasted at all bad going down, but after about five minutes he had felt sick and had rushed to the bathroom. It had been terrible.

When he had finally come out, his father was sitting there, grinning.

eight

Mike stared out at the fog.

There wasn't a damn thing he could do now but sit here and drink and wait. Nothing was going to get to the island today or get off.

Except maybe Henry. He could make it over if he had to. He was the swimmer of the family. One day you knew that he couldn't swim a stroke and the next day you hear that he's in marathons.

It must be boring as hell. Just swimming on and on. Doing the same thing over and over. You look ahead at whatever it is you're aiming for and it's only an inch or two closer.

Mike liked things to move faster.

His mind drifted back to the old neighborhood. It was the kind of a place that never really changed much. You were born there, you got a job in the industrial valley, you married a girl who lived a couple of blocks away, you had your kids there, you died there and somebody like old man MacIntyre buried you.

Mike had been set to follow the same road, but then he'd seen this movie where the stewardess married the millionaire.

It happened in real life like that sometimes. Not often, but it did happen. You'd read about it in the newspapers. Some broad who didn't have a damn thing more than any other dame, but she had it available.

Mike had begun to think about that. Marrying money. What was sauce for the goose was sauce for the gander.

But how does a poor slob get to meet a rich broad? You sure as hell weren't going to get invited to their tea parties or their yachts.

He'd let the idea live in the back of his mind and then he'd read an article in a magazine about a small college in Florida. Stevens College was a little private school that gave rich kids who didn't have the brains, or got kicked out of other schools, the chance to pick up a sheepskin without straining themselves. They spent their mornings in classrooms studying art appreciation or some damn thing, and their afternoons outside playing tennis or riding horses and getting credits for all of it.

So for the hell of it Mike wrote to the college saying that he had a son who was interested in enrolling and how about some more information.

A pack of booklets came back, all of them full of pictures of happy people playing in the sun. And Mike found out that one semester at the place cost more than two years at the state umiversity.

So that was what it all came down to. Money. It took money to get money.

How was he going to dig up enough cash to get himself enrolled down there? For at least one semester. That was all he needed. If nothing developed by the end of a semester, then the hell with all of it. But it was worth a try.

If he got a regular job after he graduated from high school, he could save enough in a couple of years. But he wasn't really the saving kind. And he had the feeling that once he got in to the routine of working eight hours a day and a regular paycheck every week, he would forget about the whole thing.

No, there was only one way to get enough money and get it when he needed it.

He had finally decided to knock over a savings and loan office. They were usually small places and they always had cash lying around. And it was something he could carry off alone. He hadn't liked the idea of having to depend on somebody else to help him pull it off.

He had begun looking around, taking a bus out of the neighborhood, and finally he had found the right place.

The next day, he'd skipped school, slipped his dad's Saturday night special into his pocket and took the bus to the South Side.

It had been ten in the morning and dark and gloomy. He had watched the savings and loan office until there was nobody inside except two women clerks and the manager, or whatever he was, and then Mike had crossed the street. He had slipped the nylon stocking over his head, stepped inside and told them it was a stickup.

All three of them had been scared silly and they fell all over themselves finding money to stuff into the paper bag which he'd brought along.

When they ran out of money, he had herded them into a back room and told them not to call the cops for fifteen minutes because he might just decide to stick around that long. Then he had closed the door, slipped off the stocking and stepped back out into the street.

He had gotten to the bus stop just as a bus pulled up. He had ridden to a transfer point and then switched buses. He hadn't heard any police sirens and so he had guessed that the people back there had really waited out the fifteen minutes.

When Mike reached home, he had gone to the loft and counted the money. Nearly seven thousand dollars.

Hell, he must have hit them at just the right time. It had damn near made him dizzy. Seven thousand bucks for a few minutes work. Maybe he should forget about college.

But he had come to his senses. Sure, he had gotten away with it this time and maybe he could do the same a few more times. But something could always go wrong and would. Some cop car would just happen to pass at the wrong time, or a clerk would push an alarm button, or a dozen things.

No, this was his first job and it would be his last. Unless maybe things didn't work out at Stevens College.

It had been tempting to spend some of the money right then and there. Maybe just a few hundred. Get some clothes. Maybe a good second-hand car. But people who knew him would begin wondering where he got the money. They might begin making good guesses, and he didn't want any of that.

So he had hidden the bills up in the rafters and kept his mouth shut.

After he graduated from high school, Mike had loafed through the summer, and then taken a Greyhound bus to Florida. Down there he looked around to see what everybody else was wearing and bought himself new clothes.

Mike had been a little nervous that the college might somehow know about his background and not take him, but the people in the bursar's office hardly even bothered to look at the transcript of his high school grades. They were more interested in the cashier's check.

He had no trouble at all fitting into campus life. He'd bought himself a convertible on time payments and he had let anybody who might be curious know that his dad was a stockbroker. In those days he didn't know what a stockbroker was, except that it sounded about right.

The first girl he'd dated had been Angie Wallace, whose father was a psychiatrist in Birmingham. Mike knew that psychiatrists earned a lot of money and for a while he was tempted to get something really going with Angie. But he thought it over. Suppose he married Angie? Then what?

After the old man got over the shock of not having a rich son-in-law, he would probably make the best of it, but the best of it to him would probably mean making sure that Mike finished college. Maybe he'd even get pushed into a medical school. That would mean years of hard bookwork and that wasn't why Mike had come there in the first place.

And then there had been Sherry, who said her father was an artist in California. Mike had never heard of him before, but Sherry said that he got thousands of dollars for each painting.

Sherry also said that her father was in his early seventies and not feeling too well. Mike had been interested, figuring that the old man must have piled up a few bucks in his time, but then he learned that he had also been married four times, had nine kids and a half dozen grand-

56

children.

Imagine what a mess that would be when he died--a bunch of ex-wives and kids all making a grab for their share of the loot. No deal.

There had been other girls, and then Myra.

Not that she was exactly the bottom of the barrel, but she was the kind of girl that you hardly ever noticed until you stepped on her. She was quiet, mousey and lonely. As far as Mike could see, she had no friends, not even girl friends.

Mike had taken her to a tavern off-campus and they had had a few beers and she had begun talking. It was like that with the quiet ones. Once they found someone who would listen, they'd begin talking and they'd tell you everything there was to know about themselves.

Myra's father was Fergusson of Fergusson Construction. And Fergusson Construction, according to Myra, was one of the biggest firms of its kind in the states. Her father had all kinds of state and federal contracts and his firm built bridges and roads all over the map.

Myra was an only child and her mother had died years ago. Her father had tried to make life as easy as he could for her, but somehow she never did have many friends and she really wasn't too good with school work either and that's why he had sent her down here.

Her father, Myra said, wasn't really an engineer. At least not one of those who had a certificate to prove it. He'd quit high school to go to work, and he had brains. He'd started practically at the pick and shovel level, but hard work had made him what he was today.

Mike had listened and thought, hell, this is it.

He'd let Myra drink three bottles of beer and that had been enough to get her a little high. Then he drove her down to the beach and the moonlight and found a spot under some palm trees and parked.

After that night, Myra almost hung around his neck, but Mike put up with it and watched the calendar.

Sure enough, she finally came to him scared--wondering how he would take it--and saying that she thought that she was pregnant and should she get an abortion?

Mike had said no and that he certainly wasn't the kind of a man who would desert a girl in trouble. Besides, he was going to ask her to marry him anyway, and this just made it sooner. Hell, he'd never seen anybody so happy in his life.

Mike told her that it might be a good idea if they got married first and then surprised her father.

Myra had been nineteen and that had been old enough for a woman to be married without parental permission, but Mike hadn't been so sure about men. He was only eighteen and he thought there might be some trouble, so he told the justice of the peace that he was twenty-two.

The justice probably didn't give a damn one way or another, because he never even asked to see their driver's licenses.

After the ceremoney, Mike and Myra took a plane north to break the news to her father.

The old man had a big place in the country-just like you saw in the movies. Lots of grass and flowers and acres of trees, and servants.

Myra's father had been in his fifties, just about average, but built solid. I'll probably look like that when I get to be his age, Mike had thought when he first saw him.

Myra had come right out with it and in one sentence told her father that she was married and pregnant.

The old man hadn't looked surprised. He'd just taken the cigar out of his mouth, looked them both over and said, "Myra, I'd like to talk to your husband alone for a few minutes."

After Myra left the room, the old man had settled himself in an arm chair. "Well, let's hear a little about your background."

Mike had cleared his throat. "My dad's a stockbroker."

The old man had chuckled. "Like hell he is. He works in a tannery. Labor."

Mike had been caught off-balance. How the hell did he know that?

The old man had been pleased with himself. "Myra wrote to me about you practically the first night she met you, I guess. She didn't tell me everything that was happening, but I didn't have to read between the lines to see that she was crazy about you. I wanted to find out a little more. So I hired private detectives."

He had looked Mike over again. "At least you look bright enough. What are you doing at a dum-dum college like Stevens?"

Just how much did the old man really know? Mike had wondered. He gave it another try. "Actually the whole thing was a mistake. I'd never heard of Stevens before, but my father read about it and he wanted me to give it a try. But now that I know what kind of a place it is, I'm switching to the state university back home after this semester. I'll be taking civil engineering."

The old man hadn't been impressed. "So you want to become an engineer? You want to put in four or five years at some diploma factory just to get a piece of paper telling you that you're an engineer? And then what?"

"I'll get a job, sir."

The old man had snorted. "I hire engineers by the dozen. There's nothing special about engineers. Hell, boy, I expected Myra to get married some day and maybe the sooner the better. But she didn't have to marry money and I don't give a damn about family. So relax, boy, I'm not going to kick you out of here."

The old man had offered him a cigar. "You might as well forget about wasting all that time in some damn school. You'll be working with me. I'm not starting you at the bottom, but I'm not making you a vice president either."

That had been just about what Mike had hoped to hear, but he had thought it might still be a good idea if he dragged his feet just a little. "Sir, I don't know anything at all about engineering."

The old man had thought that funny. "What you need to know you'll learn by watching and listening to me. The company isn't a bunch of damn engineers. It's a business and I could be making toilet seats. What you'll really need to know is how to handle people and damn near none of them will be engineers. The government, all the way from the city and county levels to the federal, is going to be your customer and that means you got to learn how to make people in power happy. And it isn't as simple as buying them. There are a lot more honest men in this world than most people think. You got to learn to bend them and make them think it was their idea all along."

The old man took the cigar out of his mouth. "There's one other thing. Myra's just a little simple, or haven't you noticed? Either that, or she just doesn't quite fit into this world. So take care of her."

The next morning, Mike and the old man had gone golfing. Mike had played only once before in his life and then on a public course. He'd rented his clubs--a driver, three irons and a putter--and he'd had to wait two hours before he could get on the course. So at the end of the eighteen holes, he'd said, the hell with it.

But the old man didn't go to public courses and he gave Mike a bag with fourteen clubs. And at the country club they didn't have to wait for anybody or anything. By the time they had finished eighteen, the old man was calling him Mike instead of boy.

The old man gave them a honeymoon in the Caribbean and when they got back, he had put Mike in an office right next to his own. Not that Mike spent much time there. Mostly he'd be in the old man's office listening and drinking scotch. Or the both of them would be off someplace selling Fergusson Construction and that meant treating the customers to a lot of hunting and fishing. Mike didn't care paarticularly about fishing, but he took to hunting. He began collecting trophies.

Mike had been worried when Henry was born. Would the old man go ga-ga over the kid like some grandfathers did? Would Mike become an outsider now that the old man had a grandson with genuine Fergusson blood inside him?

When the hospital had phoned and said it was a boy, Mike and the old man had gone down there together. They'd stood at the window of the nursery while a nurse held Henry up for inspecion. Henry had weighed just a little more than five pounds and looking at him you couldn't be impressed. You had the feeling that the kid was never going to amount to much.

The old man had felt that way too. "Well," he'd said, "I guess he takes after his grandmother's side of the family. She was just a shade over five feet." Then he had brightened. "The next one ought to be bigger."

But there wasn't going to be any next one, Mike had already decided. There wouldn't even have been a first if he hadn't thought it was necessary.

They had dropped into Myra's room for a fifteen minute visit and then gone off for a round of golf with some supervisors.

Mike's mind returned to the present.

He took a slug of his drink and looked out at the rain and the fog again.

He wondered how tigers liked weather like this.

nine

Eve turned off the night light and lay back on the bed. Her hand stretched out in the darkness to touch the knitting bag on the table--to assure herself that it was there and within reach.

She closed her eyes.

It seemed so long ago. How her mother had glared at her. "You think you're better than anybody else. It's in your eyes. The way you look at people. At me. Like we're not important. You take after your father."

Eve had watched her. "But you don't know who my father is."

Her mother's face had gotten redder. "I told you I don't know his name, but I remember what he looked like. He was ugly and stupid and drunk."

And you were with him only one night, Eve had thought. You would never have told me even that much except that you wanted to hurt.

No, Eve thought, Mama couldn't really remember who my father had been. Not just his name, but even what he looked like. She couldn't have remembered because she had probably been drunk, like she was every night.

How had it happened?

Yes, he had probably been drinking. Mama must be right about that. But not drunk like those truck drivers, or the linemen, or the construction workers. Just drinking. And he had worn a suit and a topcoat and a hat. Not a jacket and a cap.

Something must have gone wrong in his life or he would never have been drinking and he would never

62

have stopped at that cocktail bar with the row of motel units behind it. That's where it must have happened. At some motel.

He had been drinking, yes. Had it been because of something happening at the office? No, that couldn't have been it. He would have known how to handle problems like that. No, it would have had to be some kind of a personal problem.

He would have been about thirty-five. An executive. He would have been married. But there were no children. None. Ever. And it would have been his wife who had driven him to drink that evening.

His wife didn't really fit into his world. He had married her when he had been very young. It had been a mistake.

Father had money, of course. And he was handsome and intelligent. But more than that, he had hundreds of years of Family. Statesmen and senators and generals.

Father and his wife had had their quarrels. From the beginning, and then more and more often. He had tried to keep the marriage going. Yes, of course he would, because he was a gentleman. But finally he had seen how impossible it all was and he had asked his wife for a divorce.

But she wouldn't give him a divorce. At least not without a lot of trouble and scandal. She knew when she had a good thing and she wasn't going to give it up easily. And she was going to make him suffer for seeing her as she really was.

Yes, he had been drinking after his latest quarrel with his wife. He had gotten into one of his big cars and driven off. Just driven and driven, not knowing where he was going. And finally he had pulled in at the cocktail lounge because he wanted another drink.

Had Eve's mother been working behind the bar? Or had she just been sitting there on a barstool? Waiting for someone? Anyone?

It must have been quite late in the evening. Mama would have had a lot of drinks by then.

Yes, that was the way it had been. She had had plenty to drink before she had even talked to him. Otherwise she would have remembered him. She would never have forgotten him if she hadn't had so much to drink.

She had sidled up to him and begun talking. He had been tired and not thinking, and after a few more drinks, he had just shrugged and thought why not and they had gone off to one of the motel rooms behind the building.

He had wakened at three in the morning. The moonlight had been streaming through the small window. He had looked down at Eve's mother sleeping. And snoring. Yes, her mother snored. And he had not really remembered whether anything at all had happened, or whether he had just passed out.

And he had felt disgusted about the whole thing and he had quietly put on his clothes. He had put a twenty dollar bill on the dresser and he had left Mama still sleeping and driven off in his car.

Eve sighed.

How many times had Mama been married? Did she know herself? And how many men had she just lived with?

The first one Eve could remember had been redheaded and drank a lot and finally took off when Eve was five or six.

There had been others. Some she could remember only vaguely. And Eve had learned to keep away from them all. Especially when they were drinking, and they all seemed to drink.

Finally her mother had married Eddie. Really married him. Eve had been ten. How her mother had met Eddie or why he had married her, Eve never could understand. Her mother had been really lucky that time.

Eddie didn't drink or run around and he had a good steady job with the construction company. And he tried to be nice to Eve. Not in the way the others had. He had tried to treat her like she was his own daughter, but it was too late by then. She didn't want to be touched and so Eddie didn't.

But he had been proud of her. Really proud. He would look at her report card and say, "Damn, look at all them A's. And she never missed one day of school this semester."

He would show the card to Eve's mother, but Mama didn't give a damn.

Eve had been twelve years old when her mother died. It had been a cold windy day and the back steps had been icy. Eve had been at the kitchen window and she had seen it happen. Her mother had been coming home from the tavern. She had slipped and her head had struck the cement stairs.

Eve had taken care of making the burial arrangements because Eddie didn't know how to handle things like that.

There really hadn't been much of a funeral. Just a few people from Eddie's side of the family. Nobody had known who to notify about her mother.

Eve had taken over the cooking and the housework. Eddie had thought about getting a woman to come in and help, but Eve said no, she could handle it by herself.

The company picnic.

That had been six months later.

She had gone along with Eddie, but she hadn't been at all eager, because she had been taken there the year before and she knew what to expect.

Everything would be free--the hotdogs, the hamburgers, the ice cream, the candy, the beer. Everything free, but most of the people would act as though they were afraid everything would run out before they got their share. So they would eat and drink and stuff themselves and by early afternoon they would begin to get sick and the picnic grounds restrooms would be an awful mess. At five o'clock, when the stands closed up and everything was at least officially over, the kids would be sunburned and cranky and their mothers would be yelling and swearing.

She and Eddie had gotten to the picnic grounds at ten in the morning and Eddie had gone on to the horseshoe pits.

Eve had decided that she might just as well have a soda. She had gotten a bottle of orange and some of the boys at the stand had tried to talk to her, but she had walked away until she had found a quiet spot in a corner of the grounds where she had settled down under a tree to wait for five o'clock.

From there she had watched the people crowding at

the stands, and the baseball games in the distance, the footraces, and things like that, but she hadn't been really interested.

Mostly she had watched the cars come and leave the field used as a parking lot. The bigger cars belonged to the company executives, the engineers and the top supervisors, who would show up for only about an hour. They would have a couple of beers and shake hands and then they would leave. Usually their wives didn't come with them. Nor their children.

At two in the afternoon, Mike's car had pulled into the lot and Laurie had been with him. Eve had known who they were because she had seen them at the picnic the year before, but she had never talked to either one of them or particularly wanted to.

Eve had watched Mike get out of the car and she could tell from the careful way that he handled himself that he must have been drinking before he got there. He and Laurie had begun to circulate around, probably asking everybody how they were enjoying the picnic and how were the wife and the kids.

Eve had seen Mike drink a couple steins of beer and then she had noticed he suddenly became quiet and not smiling. He just nodded when people talked to him and he kept looking past them as though he was searching for something.

He had gradually worked himself away from the crowd to the edge of the picnic grounds.

Eve had realized what was the matter. The beer hadn't set too well with what he'd had to drink before.

But the president of a company can't just throw up in front of his people. So he had sneaked off and was now looking for a private place among the trees and bushes where he could be sick.

It hadn't been too bad. Just beer and maybe some whiskey came out, because he probably hadn't eaten anything that day yet.

When he was through, he had wiped his eyes and his mouth and said, "Whew!" and then "Damn!" Then he had looked up and seen Eve.

His face had gotten red and he'd quickly said, "The flu. I think I picked up the flu bug. My doctor told me not to drink anything, but I thought just one lousy little beer wouldn't hurt. I guess I was wrong."

Eve had nodded politely and said nothing.

He had stood there embarassed, not knowing what to say next, but then finally, "Do you know who I am?"

She had nodded again.

Eve had felt that she could almost read his mind. He was wondering whether it would be the wrong thing to offer her a couple of dollars to forget the whole thing. Or would that just make matters worse.

So Eve had said, "I won't tell anybody. There's no point in telling anybody."

He had stood there, staring at her, and frowning, and thinking. "How old are you?"

"Thirteen."

"Your father works for Fergusson Construction?"

"My father is dead. But my stepfather works for the company. He's a truck driver."

"What's his name?"

"Eddie Demster."

Mike had kept staring at her, but it hadn't bothered Eve. If he tried anything, she could just scream and there were a lot of people near. But at the same time, she knew that nothing was going to happen. He just wanted to look at her and try to figure out why she interested him so much.

Finally he had said, "A lot of flu going around these days."

"Yes," Eve had said.

Mike had gone back to the stands, looking back over his shoulder twice before he got there.

At three-thirty, she had seen him go to Laurie, pointing at his wristwatch. He had probably said--loud so that everybody around could hear--that it was nice to see her having such a good time, but that they'd promised to be somewhere else, and they were late already, so they'd better leave.

When Mike had gotten back to his car, he had looked

back once more to the trees where Eve still sat.

Two weeks later, Eddie had been promoted to dispatcher. He hadn't really wanted the job, but it had meant a raise in pay and so he felt that he couldn't turn it down. "Just out of the blue," he had said. "The boss himself came down and told me. I didn't think he even knew that I was alive. But he said I had a good record as a steady worker and it was about time I got promoted. He even took me out for a couple of beers."

Eddie had nodded happily. "We talked about all kinds of things. I told him about how good you're doing in school."

When Thanksgiving came near, all of the people at Fergusson Construction--but probably not the executives and the top supervisors, of course--were given free turkeys.

Eddie got his, but on the evening before Thanksgiving, the front doorbell rang and Eddie had gone to answer it.

Eve had been doing her homework on the dining room table and she had looked up when she recognized Mike's voice.

He had stood in the doorway holding a big grocery bag. "Eddie, I heard that there was some kind of mix-up about your turkey this year and you didn't get one. We can't have one of our best people thinking we forgot him."

Eddie had scratched is head. "But I got my turkey, Mr. Hegan. There wasn't any mix-up."

Mike had rubbed his chin and then smiled. "Well, I guess you might just as well take this one too. I don't know what to do with it. Just consider it a bonus."

Eddie had invited him to step inside, of course, and said, "How about a drink? I've got some beer in the refrigerator."

Eddie had gone into the kitchen for the beer and while he was away. Mike had looked at her and then frowned as if he were trying to remember. "Your face looks just a little familiar."

Eve had said, "You saw me at the picnic."

He had nodded as though it had suddenly come to

him. "I had the flu." He looked toward the kitchen. "I suppose you told your stepfather all about it?"

"No. I didn't tell him. Or anybody."

Eddie had come back with two cans of beer and he and Mike talked about baseball and things like that.

Eve had returned to her homework. Almost every time she looked up, she had found Mike watching her.

A couple of weeks later, there had been an accident at the gravel pit. There had been rain and it had frozen on the road. One of the big trucks slid out of control and it had pinned Eddie against a wall and crushed his chest.

Eddie's funeral had been a simple one. Just the few relatives that Eve knew of and some neighborhood friends and people who worked with him came to the services. Mike was one of them.

He had driven her back to the house and let her off. "I suppose now you'll be staying with relatives?"

"I don't have any relatives."

"But you can't live here alone."

"No. I don't think I'd be allowed to because I'm a minor."

"Then what's going to happen to you?"

"I don't know yet. There was a social services worker from the welfare department here yesterday and she said not to worry. Something would be arranged."

Mike had rubbed his neck. "Hell, they can't just ship you off to some orphan asylum. Let me think this over and see what I can do."

He had come back next day. "I've been talking to Laurie. That's my wife. What would you say to us adopting you? We got just one kid and there's plenty of room at the house. And Laurie would be glad to have you around."

The adoption offer had surprised her. Yes, she had been quite surprised. She had thought about it for a little while and then said yes.

Eve and Laurie had gotten along without any trouble at all. They were never close, but no trouble.

Eve had worked hard and when she graduated from high school with honors, she could have gone to a private name college in the east, but she knew what she wanted and it wouldn't be found there. Instead she had enrolled at the state university. Actually it was one of the top ten in the country and it taught the things she had wanted to learn.

So many people going to a big university are frightened to be thrown in with thousands of strangers. Once in a while they might see a face they'd known in high school, but not very often. They felt lost and insecure and lonely. Eve had seen girls break down and cry because of that.

But being alone had never bothered Eve. She had liked being anonymous, almost a number. At least that was what she preferred while she was at the university and studying.

It had been one of the requirements that first year students live on campus in a dormitory. Eve had found that most of the girls preferred to room with at least one other person, so she hadn't had any difficulty in getting assigned to a single.

But even then there had been distractions. It seemed as though most of the girls decided at one time or another to see how it felt to get drunk and sick and somebody was forever cleaning up after somebody else. Most of the time you could find a drinking or pot party somewhere down the hall and often in the hall itself.

Eve had endured it for three weeks and then told Mike that it was just too much. The noise. So he had gotten her a small apartment off-campus and bought her a car for transportation.

As far as the university was concerned, she still lived in the dorm. Every week she would drop in at the dorm two or three times to see if her room was still in one piece, to pick up her mail if there happened to be any and to be seen by the others.

She had found that the dormitory was just as noisy as ever and she had wondered how anybody could study. And probably most of them didn't, or at least not very much.

Mike had come to see her often, but they had been short visits. Mike had always seemed uneasy when he was alone with her. Talk and leave. He just wanted to see her and know that she was still there.

He had worried about her living alone. "Do you do a lot of studying in here?"

"Yes. Most of it actually."

"That's good. I mean that's why you wanted the apartment, isn't it? So you could study."

"Yes, Mike."

She had thought that she knew what he was really thinking. He was wondering if she intended to use the apartment for anything else.

He had pretended to examine the furniture. "I suppose you have a lot of dates. There are all kinds of social activities in college."

"No. I haven't had any dates. I just work."

He had wanted to believe that. "Well, that's the reason you came to college."

"Yes, Mike." She had always called him Mike. Even from the beginning. She could tell that he had never wanted her to call him Dad. Or Father.

Mike had sighed. "Well, a girl like you is bound to be asked for dates sometime, isn't she?"

"Yes. But I've been too busy."

It had been an evening two weeks later that she had first paid attention to the green Chevrolet with the dented front fender.

She had found it necessary to go back to the campus library to study. She had remained until nearly ten and then returned to the campus parking lot where she had left her car.

She had walked past the Chevrolet and there had seemed something familiar about it. An elderly man sat behind the wheel and he seemed interested in a magazine, even in that dim light.

Then she had remembered where she had seen the car before. In the parking lot behind her apartment. Her car occupied space number 25 and the Chevrolet had been parked next to it when she had left for school every morning. For the past week.

As she drove from the campus lot, Eve had kept an

eye on the rear view mirror. Yes, his headlights had flashed on and he had followed.

Eve hadn't been at all apprehensive. Actually she had been more curious than anything else.

When she had reached her apartment building and parked, she had gone inside and waited at the rear entry.

After a few moments, she had seen headlights and the Chevrolet had eased into parking space 26. The elderly man had gotten out and locked his car.

Eve had gone up to her apartment and waited at the peephole in her door. She had heard him coming up the back stairs wheezing. He had passed her door, giving it a glance, and then entered apartment 26 almost across the hall.

What now? she had wondered. Should she call the police? Was there actually any law prohibiting one person from following another? Even if there were, the old man would probably deny that he had been doing anything of the kind. And there could be complications. The police might notify the university that she was living off-campus and that could get her expelled.

No, she had decided, she would say nothing to anyone. Besides, there didn't seem to be any real danger. He was just a frail old man and she had felt that she could handle him if that ever became necessary.

The next morning she had checked the mail slots in the foyer. The old man's name appeared to be J. L. Worley

When she reached the university, she had gone to the library's reference room and consulted the town directory. She had found the entry: *Worley, John L. 183 E. Hardy St. employment Marotti Detective Agency.* The address had not been that of her apartment building.

So that was it? John L. Worley worked for a private detective agency and his latest assignment had been important enough so that he had moved into apartment 26 in her building? And obviously with the purpose of keeping an eye on her twenty-four hours a day.

Did he just stand there at his own little peephole waiting for her to leave her apartment? That seemed hardly likely. He must have some kind of a signaling device that

72

told him whenever Eve left her apartment.

When she got home that evening, Eve had listened carefully as she opened her door. Yes, the faint sound of a buzzer had come from inside apartment 26 across the hall.

The old man didn't have to spend his time at the peephole. He had rigged up a buzzer so that it sounded in his apartment every time her door was opened.

But who would want him to keep an eye on Eve?

The answer had, of course, been obvious.

Mike.

What should she do now? she had wondered. Should she go to Mike and tell him that she knew about Worley? Would he just get rid of the old man and hire someone a bit less obvious?

And if he admitted hiring Worley, what reason would Mike give? That he had just been trying to see that she was protected?

Probably. But what real protection was a frail little old man?

No. Protection wasn't the reason Mike had hired him. Mike had simply wanted to know what she was doing, and with whom. Who was she seeing? Who came to her apartment? He wanted to know.

She had sighed. There really hadn't been anything to keep Worley busy and there wasn't likely to be. Her day consisted of going to the campus and occasionally to the supermarket. She prepared her own meals in the apartment and she ate alone.

Mike was wasting his money. She had come to the university for one reason only. She wanted to get her degree and get it as fast as possible. Anything else was a distraction and she had wanted no distractions.

What should she do now that she knew about Worley? Nothing, she had decided. Absolutely nothing. If it made Mike feel better to keep tabs on her, let it be. Leave things as they were and keep quiet. And she had never mentioned a word to Mike on the subject, even to this day.

The first semester she had been asked to go out any

number of times. A few of the people had been quite persistent. But she had turned them all down. They had been boys, really.

Finally she had bought herself a wedding ring. Just a plain gold band with almost invisible diamond flakes and she had let people see it. She had talked about her invisible husband now and then and it had worked. She had been left more or less alone after that.

Whenever she had gone home on weekends, she had always remembered to slip the ring off and put it in her purse.

Eve had gotten her Bachelor of Science degree in business in only three years, and that had meant going to school summers too.

After graduation, Eve had waited a month and then gone to Mike. You couldn't just sit and wait for things to happen. That was wasting time. She had asked Mike for a job with the company.

He had grinned. "What the hell do you want with a job, Eve? You don't need to lift a finger if you don't want to."

"But I want to lift a finger." She had smiled. "After all, I did go to college and learn something about business."

He had laughed, of course. "Eve, you don't learn about business in school."

Like hell you don't, she had thought, but she had smiled again. "It's just that I like to keep busy. And going to parties or playing tennis doesn't seem to be enough."

And so Mike had been magnanimous and had put her in the company's accounting department. She had been given the title of coordinator and an office of her own. She had even been offered a secretary, but she had turned that down. Too much was too much.

Mike had probably told Sterling, the head of the department, to send a little work her way now and then. Nothing complicated or important. Just something that she could sign or okay. It had all been make-work and Eve had known that it would be that way.

But the title of coordinator had enabled her to wander

about and look at things and be absent from her own office for hours at a time. Even days.

She could wander into any department and look at anything. Any books, any figures, and she could ask questions. She made it a point never to get into anyone's way and so she had been tolerated and humored because she had been a threat to no one's job, or ego, or macho.

She had had coffee, and cokes, and maddening small talk with everyone and anyone. she had really become quite popular. She had let people call her Eve and she had smiled and smiled and smiled.

But God how she had really been working--learning what there was to know, learning what the company had been, what it was now and what it might be in the future.

She had taken pains not to let anyone suspect what she was really doing. She had even sneaked back to the office on weekends when there had been nobody around except a few maintenance people. Really, it had been almost like going back to college and working for a master's degree.

And all of it had been right there to learn, to absorb. In the company's books. That was where the center, the heart, the brain of the company lay. In the office records, in the filing cabinets, in the vaults.

She had, of course, found it necessary to learn at least something about the technical aspects of the work done in the field. But it had not been really necessary to know a great deal. Just enough so that she had a general idea of what the engineers were doing. No, the important part of the company was knowing what things were going to cost, and where to get them, and how to end up with as much as you could get on the bottom line.

Eve had confirmed what she had always suspected. Mike knew very little about the company's business. He had had no training at all. After his father-in-law's death, he had simply moved into the bigger office and been given more important things to sign. Other people really made the decisions. The department heads, the specialists, the men in the field. Perhaps it had been just luck, but the company was running itself. Mike was no more than a figurehead.

Was he aware of that?

It had been so tempting to go to him and tell Mike that she could run the whole damn company and know exactly what she was doing.

But no. That wasn't the way to do things. And so she had bided her time. Tapped her foot. Yes, and worried about the company. Suppose Mike did something stupid and brought everything down like a house of cards? She had held her breath, and so far, at least, everything still seemed to be functioning.

When Eve had heard that Mrs. Jenson, Mike's secretary was retiring, she had gone to him. "Why don't you let me have the job?"

He hadn't taken her seriously. "That's a big step down from coordinator."

No it isn't, Eve thought. Not if you know how important Mrs. Jenson was to the firm.

Mike had turned her down. "This is no job for you, Eve. You don't want to be just hired help. Besides, I've already hired a new secretary."

And that had been Oriana.

She had dark, almost black eyes and raven hair. She was quiet and pale and she too seemed to watch and wait.

Oriana was something of a mystery. Even today. They had exchanged almost no personal talk. All that Eve really knew about Oriana was that she had been born here on this island.

Eve had known almost immediately that Oriana and Mike were having an affair. She had waited clinically for it to disintegrate. But it hadn't.

Mike had even introduced Oriana into the household. Laurie must have known what was going on. Yes, but she even seemed to approve of Oriana.

Eve thought she knew why.

ten

Oriana made herself stop thinking about Pitts and the tiger.

She would think about Ben Williams and his wife, Odie, and how they had been the caretakers at the big house when the Forrests were off the island and that had been almost all of the time. As a matter of fact, Oriana couldn't remember ever seeing any of them at all.

When she had been a little girl, Oriana had made her way over to the Forrest place as often as she could. Ben and Odie were both tall and dark and they had always been kind to her.

Sometimes Oriana would eat supper with them in their kitchen and help with the dishes and later she would wander through the beautiful rooms of the house unitl dark. Then she would join Odie and Ben outside where they would all sit in high-backed wicker chairs.

It had been so nice out there and Odie would have a pitcher of lemonade on the side table. Ben had read almost every book in the Forrest library, especially the family histories, and so he would talk about the island people who had lived and died there as though he knew all of them personally.

"It was at the turn of the century," Ben would say, "by that I mean 1801 and afterwards, when the Pitot sisters went off to Europe after their father had died to look at art and statues and when they came back six years later, they had this Prussian with them. He was married to Amelia, I believe. Or was it Rosette?"

Odie, who had done a lot of listening to Ben would say, "It was Amelia. Though some said it was both. Maybe it didn't make much difference. Amelia was in her middle fifties and Rosette wasn't but a year younger. And the Baron must have been about their age too, give or take a year of two."

Ben would nod. "His name was Von Something, but everybody just called him the Baron or the Prussian. The Pitot place was on the northern tip of the island. Not one of the bigger places, but a tidy plantation. Some forty or fifty souls, all counted. Well, when the Pitot sisters went off to Europe for the grand tour, they had left Mr. Meekins, their overseer, in charge of everything. They were in Europe six years and they might have stayed there forever, except that the money from home ran dry and they had to come back, which they did with this Prussian whom one of them had married a month before sailing.

"The Baron had been in the Prussian army all his life and was now retired and he played the flute. Two hours a day, come rain or shine, while facing in the direction of Berlin."

"Now, Ben," Odie would say. "You're inventing that Berlin part."

Ben would shrug. "Anyway, he practiced two hours a day, and when he and the sisters came back to Pitot Point, they found the place pretty well messed up--all run down and the only one seeming to benefit being Meekins who probably had a bank account in Switzerland or wherever they stashed loot in those days. So the Prussian not only fired him, but challenged him to a duel.

"Actually it wasn't so much of a challenge. More like an ultimatum. Meekins had the choice of getting shot right then and there or going through with the duel and hoping. So they had their duel and the Prussian shot Meekins right between the eyes.

"It made a scandal on the island--not because it was a duel, there having been a few of those before--but because the Prussian had dueled with an overseer and a thing like that could ruin the social structure. Also the people here didn't like the fact that the seconds for the duel had been slaves who probably didn't give a damn who got the bullet between his eyes anyway.

"Something drastic might have been done about the Prussian then and there, but the Pitots were related to the Websters, the Crandalls and the de Brosses, and Meekins wasn't related to nobody. So Meekins was buried and the Prussian decided to run the Pitot place without no overseer at all, which raised more eyebrows.

"In those days all the overseers and the gentry rode horses. But the Prussian didn't think much of horses. He claimed that there wasn't a more stupid animal on the face of the earth than a horse, him having learned that when he was in the Prussian cavalry. Also he said that riding a horse gave the horse all of the exercise and he was damned if he was going to waste any more of his life giving a horse exercise. All this didn't do anything to make him popular here, the island folks thinking so high about their horses and knowing more about their blood lines than they did about their own family tree.

"It wasn't but a year or two before the Pitot place was shining and cleaner than any other on the island, and it looked like the Prussian was cropping about twice as much cotton per acre as anybody else. Which made the island wives look at their husbands and their sons and wonder why they spent so much time riding, and hunting, and drinking instead of overseeing their overseers for a little more production and money.

"The Prussian, who didn't drink a lick and never went hunting, gave all of the people on Pitot Point a rank, like private, corporal or sergeant, depending on their character and how hard they worked. Island folks could stand for that, but when he promoted one of his slaves to second lieutenant, they thought he'd gone too far, figuring that no slave should hold a commission, no matter whose private army it was."

Ben would re-light his long cigar. "In those days every free gentlewoman would do things like painting and music, but not very much. It was just to keep them genteel and occupied on rainy afternoons.

"The Pitot sisters weren't no exceptions, at least not until the Prussian came along. Amelia played the harp and Rosette the harpsichord. They could play about seven or eight pieces, some of them together, and that was about all.

"Practically the first thing the Prussian did when they got here was to set the Pitot sisters to practicing their instruments regular. Two hours a day, which was more than they'd done in a month before. And he made them walk three miles a day, real brisk, claiming it improved their legs, lungs and disposition. And he made them take German lessons, which he administered.

"He also figured that it was simpler to teach the slaves German than it was for him to learn English, especially the kind they spoke, which was Gullah. From what I read, they took to it eager, though not always good. The Prussian also financed one of those German pastors to come over and teach them Lutheran, but the pastor landed in Savannah first and decided to stay there. He never did repay the Prussian for the boat ride from Europe.

"Well, things went on at a good pace, the Pitot place getting neater and fatter, the sisters improving their music, lungs and complexions, and the slaves singing *lieders,* when suddenly the Prussian announced that he was freeing all his slaves.

"The island didn't take to that at all. Here and there in the south, some people were freeing their slaves--usually in their wills, because who's going to free a slave while you're still alive to use him--but it had never been done on the island before and everybody was afraid it might be catching and cause discontent.

"The Prussian wasn't no late humanitarian, he just didn't think that slavery was efficient. He said that no slave is going to work when he's not being watched and you can't watch forty people at one time. So he freed all his slaves and then hired them back on wages and they had to produce or leave. Also he charged them rent for their cabins. It wasn't much, but just enough to remind them who still owned the place, freedom or no freedom.

"The island people had thoughts of having the Prussian declared insane or at least a man of loose morals. There was even serious talk about burning down the Pitot house-not that the gentry themselves would do anything like that--but they'd look the other way if their overseers got together and did the job.

"Well, the Prussian seemed to know about the talk and what plans were being made because he had a spy system, most of which spoke some German.

"Pitot Point used to have a wharf jutting right out into the ocean, like at Deveraux house, and ocean schooners would dock right there to pick up the cotton. So that year after the Prussian harvested his crop and loaded it on the ship, he also packed up every scrap of furniture in Pitot house--including the harp and harpsichord. Then, while playing his flute, he marched all his employees and their families aboard."

"Now, Ben," Odie would say, "There's no place where it says he was playing the flute."

Ben would shrug. "Well, the ship stopped off at Savannah for a couple of hours while the Prussian went ashore to beat up a German pastor, and then it went right up to New York where he sold his cotton and gave everybody good severence pay.

"As for the Prussian and the Pitot sisters, they went on to someplace in Pennsylvania, where he could understand the language, and settled down to gentleman farming. The three of them began giving concerts every Sunday afternoon in their parlor and the recitals was always well attended. They all lived on into their nineties and died peacefully in their sleep."

Oriana had asked Ben if he had ever seen her father.

Ben had nodded. "He was a nice-looking man. Tall, with black hair. A real gentleman."

"My mother never tells me anything about him and I don't remember him at all. He died when I was about three years old and he's buried in the Deveraux cemetery behind the house. I put flowers on his grave."

Odie had sighed. "Your mama don't talk to you much, does she child?"

"No. Not much. We live below the stairs in the kitchen and one other room. The rest of the house is empty and there's no furniture or anything and the windows are mostly blown out or broken."

"What does your mama do with her time?" Odie had asked.

"Mostly she just sits and stares out of the window and waits for five o'clock. Then she drinks brandy and plays solitaire and goes to bed."

There had been silence for a while and then Oriana had said, "My mother's maiden name was Chapman. Was there a Chapman plantation?"

Ben had nodded. "Yes. But things went downhill for the Chapmans--just like they did for everyone else after a while. They had to leave and they settled in Raleigh where your Chapman grandfather got himself a job selling insurance. Your mother was about fourteen then. I heard that they lived in a three-room apartment over a drugstore."

"If Mama was off the island, how did she and my father ever get to meet?"

"Your daddy went off to college somewhere near Raleigh and he looked up the Chapmans, since they were island people too. And what with one thing and another and your father not particularly liking college anyway, the two of them got married and came back to the island."

Ben would think about it for a while. "Your father and your mother lived with your Deveraux grandparents at the Deveraux place. It was still a working plantation then, though barely. But your mother liked it and I heard that she swore she'd never leave the island again, come what might.

"Time passed. More families left the island and then Grandpa and Grandma Deveraux both died in the same year. Six months later, your father broke his neck when his horse fell while trying to jump a stone fence and that left you and your mama alone, with you about three at the time.

"When the estate was settled, there wasn't much of Deveraux left. Just the house and a few acres. Your mother sold most of those right away and she bought the brandy."

Ben would smile. "Four hundred twenty cases of brandy. When they came to island, she hired me to haul them from the wharf to Deveraux house. Four hundred twenty cases. I guess she just wanted to make sure that she had enough brandy to last her the rest of her life. Has she got any left, Oriana?"

"Yes. But I never counted them."

Oriana had been twelve when Ben died. He had been just a little sick for a few days and then he had quietly died.

Odie had gotten some help and a minister from the mainland and they buried Ben in the Forrest plot behind the house. Then Odie had packed up and decided to move in with one of her sisters on the mainland.

Oriana had been with her at the wharf while they waited for the boat to come.

Odie had been sad. "Child, what's going to become of you?"

Oriana had tried to keep from crying. "Now take care of yourself, Odie."

When Odie was gone, that left only Pitts on the Forrest plantation and Oriana didn't want to have anything to do with him.

But she would sneak up close to the house and look at it from the cover of the woods for hours and dream about being inside once again.

She had supposed that the Forrests couldn't get anybody to replace Ben and Odie, or they didn't care, or they thought that having Pitts around was enough, because no one else ever came to the house.

Oriana had thought that Pitts would move into the big house itself, like Ben and Odie had done, but he still slept in his cabin and whenever he came out, he would grunt and swear and throw an empty bottle on the trash heap.

And then one evening when she knew that Pitts had just finished another bottle and wouldn't be up for a long while, she had come out of the woods into the bright moonlight to the back of the big house and let herself in.

It had been so bright through the long windows that she could see everything inside. She had wandered all over the house again, touching the covered furniture and running her fingers along the marble of the big fireplaces. She had gone up to the second floor and even the third where the servants had once lived.

She had felt that all of this was really hers now because anybody who cared for it was dead now or gone away. She had liked to come sweeping down the main staircases and she had almost heard chamber music from somewhere in the house when she did.

After that evening, she had come back to the Forrest house whenever there was moon enough to see by and she knew that Pitts was drunk and sleeping.

But sometimes when Pitts didn't have a bottle, he wouldn't go to sleep. He would just prowl around the grounds cursing and she didn't dare come out of the woods.

There had come the time when there had been so much moonlight that she just had to see the inside of the house again. So she had stolen a bottle of brandy from Mama's cellar and left it right at the doorway of Pitts' cabin where he was bound to step on it when he came out. And she waited.

At first he must have thought it was a snake, because he jumped when his foot touched it. Then he looked carefully and picked up the bottle. He had looked at it and then all around and even at the sky. Then he had taken the bottle inside the cabin.

Oriana had waited until she could hear him snoring and then she sneaked into the big house again.

The next evening she had left another bottle beside Pitts' cabin and had watched him drink it while he sat in the doorway.

The third night she had seen Pitts hiding near the cabin waiting to see who was leaving the bottle, so she had just thrown it out on the soft ground near him and then run deeper into the woods and waited.

Of course she should have known that it couldn't go on that way because there were just Pitts and Oriana and her mother on the island.

Pitts had come over to Deveraux early the next evening when the sun was still up and he had had that dirty smile on this face when he talked to Mama.

Mama was about halfway through her bottle by then and she hadn't been able to understand why Pitts was there and she didn't really care. She just wanted to finish the bottle and go to sleep.

But Oriana had known what it was all about and why he was standing there looking at Mama. He thought that she was leaving the bottle for him and he thought that she wanted him. But Mama didn't care about those things any more.

Pitts had come closer and closer to Mama and Oriana had known what was going to happen if nothing was done. So she had gone into the bedroom for the double-barreled shotgun. She had found some dusty shells and put them into the chambers.

Then she had stepped back into the kitchen and said, "Leave my Mama alone," and she had fired the first barrel past his head where it had caused a lot of pieces of tabby to fly from the open doorway.

The recoil of the shotgun had almost torn it from her hands, but she had hung on and told Pitts that if he didn't get out of there right away the next shot would get him in the belly.

He had run away and she had quickly put another shell into the chamber that had been fired and waited, but he didn't come back.

All that time her mother had just sat there and stared. Then she had poured more brandy and started another solitaire game.

Months had passed and Oriana had stayed home at Deveraux. But one night there had been a perfect moon again and she just couldn't stand being away from the Forrest house. The wind had been so soft and the fireflies thick. So she had gone back through the woods to look at the Forrest house once more.

She had stared at it and wondered where Pitts was and what he was doing. Maybe he had gotten a bottle or two from the mainland and gone to sleep. She had crept closer to his cabin and listened for his snoring.

Pitts had jumped out of the darkness of a tree and glared down at her. "What the hell are you doing here? What do you want?"

And Oriana had known that she just couldn't tell him, so she had said nothing at all.

He had stared down at her a long while. "You're just a skinny kid." But his eyes had gleamed anyway and he had pulled her close.

When it was over, she had run all the way back to Deveraux house. She had wanted to wake her mother and tell her what had happened and maybe cry.

But she had known that it wouldn't make any difference to Mama. Oriana had even thought about the shotgun and going back and killing Pitts.

But then she would be put in jail and who would take care of Mama?

So she had just washed herself over and over and then tried to go to sleep.

eleven

MacIntyre finished eating and drank his milk. He considered for a moment opening the door and putting the tray on the floor outside.

No, he decided. There's no telling what might be out there silently watching and waiting. If he opened the door even a crack, the tiger might suddenly spring and force his way in. No, he would open the door only if he heard the sound of someone's voice. That would tell him there was no tiger out there.

He adjusted the two pillows so that he was more comfortable. He should have asked Bowler to bring up something to read.

MacIntyre sighed.

His first receptionist had been Mrs. O'Brien. His mother had hired the woman herself. Mrs. O'Brien had been in her middle forties and quite hefty.

The week after MacIntyre's mother died, Mrs. O'Brien had suddenly announced that she was really needed back at home and she was quitting, but she had a daughter, Angie, who had just graduated from high school and could type forty words per minute and could handle the receptionist job just fine.

Angie O'Brien had been eighteen and she had been, well, quite well-developed and ready. You could see it, you could feel it in the air, and you could almost smell it.

It had all been obvious, of course. MacIntyre and his classmates at medical school had been warned about that sort of thing by professors who snickered. The young receptionists. They were all really out to get themselves the doctor, one way or another. And sometimes, as MacIntyre then realized, with the help of their mothers.

Angie had played it slow and cool, probably the way her mother had told her to. Don't go too fast or come on too strong or you could scare him off and ruin everything. Just be polite and friendly and smile a lot and do no more than that for at least a month.

The month had passed and MacIntyre had been able to see that stage two was now in operation. It had been almost like a change in climate. Angie's eyes were now just a little wider and she seemed to be always closer and sometimes they actually touched.

MacIntyre had found himself tingling, and nervous, and, yes, anticipating.

After two weeks, he had found himself saying, "Miss O'Brien, I wonder if you would mind staying just a little while after office hours today? There's something I'd like to check up on in our books."

"Oh?" she had said, smiling slowly. "Is there anything wrong, doctor?"

"No, no," he had said quickly. "Nothing wrong. Everything is fine, as a matter of fact. It's just that here and there are a few little things that we could perhaps straighten up."

The smile had grown intimate. "Of course, doctor. I'll be happy to stay as long as you like."

The patients MacIntyre had inherited from Dr. Walters almost never called ahead for appointments. They just barged into the office and waited until he was able to see them. As he worked that day, MacIntyre's eyes had kept going to the clock on the wall. He had found himself perspiring.

Four o'clock had come. Four-thirty. He had met Angie's eyes as he had let a patient out of his examining room. They had definitely gleamed. Almost like a satisfied cat's.

And then it had come. That sick, sick feeling in the pit of his stomach and the panic.

He hadn't really been anticipating five o'clock. He had

been dreading it. Dreading it because he knew what would really happen. Or not happen. It was all going to be just like it had been when he and Laurie had been together in the Cadillac.

Yes, exactly the same. He knew it.

He had opened the door to the reception room just a crack and peeked out. Two more patients. Two more patients and then he and Angie would be alone. He had found himself trembling violently.

He had shut the door and locked it. Damn, what was he going to do now? He couldn't really go through with it. He just couldn't. He had even thought wildly about slashing his wrists.

But then the phone had rung. That blessed phone. Angie had answered it, of course, but then she had pressed the buzzer to indicate that it was for him.

It had been Mrs. Seborg and she hated to bother him during office hours, but her mother's breathing sounded really funny and she seemed to be out of her head. Could he come over? Maybe after office hours? Or whenever he could?

And he said, yes, yes, right away. He had grabbed his bag and stopped at Angie's desk. "An emergency. I have to go out immediately."

At the door he had turned. "You'd better close the office for today, Angie. I don't think I'll be able to make it back. There's no telling how long this will take." He had hurried away.

Mrs. Seborg's mother had been one of his kidney patients and when he saw her he knew that she had lapsed into her final coma. He had told Mrs. Seborg the truth--that she could have her mother rushed to a hospital, but it really wouldn't do any good. Mrs. Seborg had agreed that hospitals were so expensive nowadays and anyway her mother wasn't under any medical plan and it was better to die at home among those who loved you.

MacIntyre had gone home and up to his room. He had lain on his bed and stared at the ceiling.

What could he do about Angie? What the devil could he do? Tomorrow would come and he had to be ready with something. Some excuse. He had thought and thought and finally came up with something.

He had gone downtown to Sears and found just what he was looking for--the photograph of a good-looking girl in an 8 X 10 picture frame. Just some model, of course, and it was a way to make the frame more attractive to customers, but it was the picture that he really wanted.

When he had gotten home, he had disguised his handwriting and written With all my love, my darling Jamie, at the base of the photograph and signed it Genevieve.

The next morning, he had gone to the office early, before Angie would be there, and he had placed the framed photograph on his desk.

When he had heard Angie in the reception room, he had quickly slipped into the bathroom and left the door open just enough to see out.

After a while Angie had come into the office to dust and straighten his desk and when she had seen the photograph and read the inscription, her mouth had dropped.

MacIntyre had stepped out of the bathroom wiping his hands on a paper towel. "Good morning, Angie." He had stopped in front of the photograph. "My fiancee, Genevieve. I've known her for years, but it wasn't until last night that we became formally engaged."

Maybe that would have been enough, but he hadn't wanted to leave Angie any hopes that she might be able to take him away from Genevieve. "Her father's in oil. Has all kinds of investments in Saudi Arabia. He's going to help me open a clinic. Finance it."

Angie had stayed through the day, very quiet, but the next morning her mother had phoned and said that Angie wasn't feeling too well, but Mrs. O'Brien was perfectly willing to fill in for her because she had discovered that she wasn't really that much needed at home after all. Maybe she could come back permanently because she didn't have any idea how long Angie might be sick. It could be months.

MacIntyre had quickly said that he was sorry, but he had made previous arrangements with another woman to come in whenever Angie might happen to be sick and he had also told this woman that if Angie should ever quit, or be sick a long time, she could have first crack at the job. MacIntyre hadn't wanted Mrs. O'Brien to come back and find out that there was no Genevieve.

MacIntyre hired one of his patients as the new reception-ist. Mrs. Landry. She was in her fifties and he knew that she could use the money because she owed plenty on her doctor bill. She had four children in school. All of them boys.

MacIntyre had continued to live with his father on the second floor of the funeral parlor. Every once in a while, his father would ask him why he didn't move--find himself a better place. He could afford one now. But Mac-Intyre had said that he just hated to move and he liked the neighborhood. Besides, he had his practice here and what was the sense of wasting a lot of time commuting from some suburb.

So MacIntyre had really settled in and he had taken up photography as a hobby.

When MacIntyre's father turned sixty, he had begun talking retirement and moving to a warmer climate where he could take it easy.

MacIntyre had never thought about that happening be-fore. Somehow you just thought that things would go on and on. But suppose his father did retire? What then? He would probably sell the building. To another mortician? Not too likely. They weren't locating in that part of town anymore.

MacIntyre had mulled it over and one evening after he had finished developing some photos in the basement dark room, he had stepped out and watched his father put the finishing touches on the body of Giardo, the shoe repairman, who had died of cancer and now weighed less than ninety pounds.

MacIntyre had cleared his throat. "I've been thinking things over, Dad. I'm not really suited for medicine."

And that had been the absolute truth. He hadn't had any real interest in medicine at all, and besides, half of his patients made him so nervous that his stomach was always tight and he knew he was going to get ulcers be-fore too much longer.

MacIntyre had continued. "The point is that a man should do what makes him the happiest."

His father had grunted. "And what makes you happiest?"

MacIntyre had felt a bit warm and spoke swiftly. "I've been thinking of giving up medicine and going to a morticians college. I'd be finished in two years and I could take over here when you retire. I'd buy the building, of course. I wouldn't expect you to just give it to me."

His father had stared at him. "You're crazy, Jamie. Absolutely looney. Damn it, right now you earn four times what I do."

"It isn't a question of money, Dad. It's just that I've been thinking this over and there's no sense in ruining my whole life doing something that I really don't want to do at all."

"Crazy," his father had said again. "Over the edge. You're a mental case."

MacIntyre had retreated back into his darkroom.

One of MacIntyre's patients had been August Bellinger, who was the ward boss and a bigwig down in city hall. After MacIntyre had given him his yearly examination and told Bellinger to go on a diet, lay off the booze and stop smoking so many cigars--none of which he would do--Bellinger had gotten dressed and said, "Jamie, how would you like to be the coroner of this great city?"

MacIntyre had blinked. "Coroner?"

"Coroner. I'll put your name on the ticket." Bellinger had grinned. "We need a name to fill in the blank space on the ticket. To tell you the truth, I been asking around without any luck. I can't find any doctor who wants to be coroner, but the law says that the coroner has to be a doctor. The job pays a thousand bucks a year, but I suppose you make that much on a weekend?"

MacIntyre had been quite interested. "What does a coroner do? I mean I know what coroners do medically, but not in the official sense."

"Not a damn thing, Jamie. We got civil service people who do all the cutting and slicing. All you'd have to do is show up at the office every week or two to sign a few papers. We could even bring them to you if you'd like that better."

MacIntyre's heart had pounded a bit. "Well, if I am

elected, I would insist upon being more than a figure-head."

"Suit yourself, Jamie. You get the title and what you do with it is your business."

The party had won the election, as usual, and Mac-Intyre had gone downtown to the Municipal Building where the morgue was located.

He had introduced himself to the assistant coroner-who wasn't a doctor, just a technologist-and his assistants. MacIntyre had told them that he was going to be more than just a figurehead, because he didn't believe in figureheads.

They had all been polite and doubtful, but he had surprised them by showing up and helping a little here and there and getting to know his department people. It wasn't long before he was dropping in three or four nights a week and they even gave him a set of keys.

MacIntyre decided that he might just as well give up the idea of going to the mortuary college after all. And when his father retired and sold the building to a plumbing contractor, MacIntyre moved to an apartment close to the Municipal Building, though he still kept his practice in the old neighborhood.

Coroner, MacIntyre now thought. He could probably be coroner the rest of his life if he wanted to.

He yawned, closed his eyes and fell asleep smiling.

twelve

It was now nearly midnight. Bowler had put it off long enough.

He felt a bit giddy as he rose from the kitchen table. Perhaps he had taken just a little too much brandy during the course of the day. He stared at the rain streaking the dark windows. Good.

Bowler slipped into his raincoat and hood. He unbolted and opened the door to the cellars under the house, switched on the light, and stepped onto the clay floor.

His eyes went immediately to the top-opening deep freezer. Hegan had brought it to the island last week and Bowler still didn't know why. The upright freezer in the kitchen certainly provided enough space for the needs of the household.

Bowler glanced at the door leading from the cellars to the world outside. Now it was closed and securely bolted. But it hadn't been this morning. It had been open because it was Clara's practice to leave it that way to provide ventilation against the dampness in the basement area.

After Bowler and Clara had been told about the tiger, they had gone back to the kitchen and locked themselves in. But then Clara had remembered about the open cellar door. She had left their kitchen and gone to close it.

She had been gone too long and Bowler had opened the door to the cellars to see what was keeping her.

He had seen the tiger. Just a few feet away.

It must have entered the cellar earlier and now it just sat there, its back to Bowler, between Clara and the door back to the kitchen.

Clara had stood beyond the tiger, her face ashen white, her eyes wide with silent terror. The tiger had stared at her, unmoving, and apparently unaware of Bowler's presence behind him.

Bowler's heart had pounded and he had felt as though he were going to faint. His first instinct had been to quickly slam the door shut, but then he had stared, frozen and fascinated by the scene before him.

Clara had stood there for the longest time and the tiger had done nothing but just watch her. Then she had slowly, ever so slowly, backed away from the tiger until she had bumped into the unused chest freezer.

Without turning to look at what she was doing, her fingers had found the lid of the freezer and she had slowly raised it.

It had been almost like watching a slow motion film. Clara had climbed into the freezer bit by bit and then, just as gradualy, she had pulled the lid down over her.

The tiger had risen to its feet and moved to the freezer. It had almost purred, apparently puzzled by Clara's disappearance, and had sniffed at the sides of the freezer.

It had leaped gracefully onto the top of the freezer, investigating its surface. And then after a full minute, seemingly bored by it all, had jumped off.

It had moved on to the still open door to the garden. Bowler had watched it lope away through the garden area and disappear into the brush.

He had run to the open door and quickly shut and bolted it.

Then he had turned and stared at the freezer. Clara was still in there. She did not know that the tiger was gone. She did not know that it was safe to come out.

His eyes had fastened hypnotically on the key in the lock of the freezer and he had moved as though in a trance. His fingers had touched the key and then quietly he had turned it. The freezer was now locked.

How long would it take Clara to asphyxiate in there? For that matter, would she asphyxiate at all? Suppose she managed to break out? Or was there a way of opening the freezer from the inside?

He had begun to perspire. He could hear no sounds from inside the freezer. Apparently she was still lying there, thinking that the tiger was still waiting.

Bowler's foot had touched the freezer's unconnected electric cord. He had picked up the plug, hesitated a moment, and the pushed it into the electric outlet. The freezer motor had begun to whir and the red operating signal light on its side had flashed on.

And then he had heard from Clara inside the chest. She had begun to pound on the lid and he had heard her muffled screams.

Could she break out of there? And if she did, what would she do to him?

He had been terrified and frantically he had begun piling cases of brandy on the top of the freezer until there had been room for no more. And all that time he had heard the pounding and the screaming.

He had fled back to the kitchen and bolted the door. He had gone on into their small bedroom and closed the door after him too. He had lain on the bed, not quite sure whether he could still hear Clara or whether it was his imagination.

He had fallen asleep. Perhaps it had been some kind of a nervous reaction which made him do that. And he had started awake after perhaps half an hour, suddenly aware that now he would have to make and serve breakfast alone. And lunch. And dinner.

At breakfast, Laurie had asked him about Clara and he told her that Clara wasn't feeling too well and that she had gone to bed. When Laurie said that she would see Clara and find out if there was anything she could do, Bowler had quickly said that Clara was asleep and besides, she was the type of a person who just wanted to be left alone when she was sick.

Laurie said that MacIntyre wasn't feeling too well either, and she sent Bowler upstairs to MacIntyre's room with a tray.

Bowler found MacIntyre's bed stripped of sheets, blankets and pillows. He wondered where MacIntyre might be and finally knocked on the bathroom door.

might be and finally knocked on the bathroom door.

MacIntyre's voice had come from inside. "What is it?"

"Breakfast, sir. I've brought up a tray."

Bowler heard the door being unlocked. It was opened just enough so that MacIntyre could receive the tray.

"Don't forget to close the French doors when you leave." The door was closed and re-locked.

Bowler saw MacIntyre's briefcase on the night table. This time it was unlocked and empty.

But it hadn't been the last time MacIntyre had come to the island. Then Bowler had finally managed to sneak into MacIntyre's room and get at the briefcase. He had always wondered what MacIntyre kept in there.

Bowler had found the right key from his ring and turned the lock. He had found the briefcase crammed with glossy 8 X 10 photographs.

And Bowler had been shocked.

How did MacIntyre do it, he had wondered. Probably some kind of a timing device. MacIntyre would set the timer and then he'd rush out there in front of the camera naked as a jay bird and all excited. And he was in every one of those damn photos.

Bowler had shuddered. He'd seen dirty pictures before in his life.

But with dead people?

thirteen

When Oriana had left the island, she had stopped off in Savannah to see a real estate agent and make arrangements to sell what was left of Deveraux. He had told her that there really wasn't any market for a property like that now, but that maybe he could unload it on one of the banks. She couldn't expect much money. Oriana had said that was all right, just sell it.

She had taken a bus north until she had found a city where she thought she would like to stay. When she had gotten off the bus, she had gone to a telephone book and copied the addresses of a half dozen of the city's business schools. She had taken a taxi to the first name on her list.

In the school office, she had asked questions and found that it was just about what she wanted and so she hadn't looked any further.

She had asked the registrar if there were any rooming houses in the neighborhood and been told that there were quite a few within walking distance.

Oriana had found the Neville place on a residential side street lined with large old homes, most of which seemed to have been converted into rooming houses and apartments.

The Nevilles had both been in their sixties, small, and smiling eagerly. They had made up their minds right away about Oriana and they had said that yes, indeed, they did have a room vacant. Alma Bergan had just graduated from cosmeticians school and gone back to her hometown to work for her aunt and maybe take over the shop when her aunt retired.

Mrs. Neville said that the room was on the third floor. It had a dormer window and used to belong to one of the servants when Mrs. Neville had been a child. It might get just a little chilly in winter, but an electric space heater came with it and they always put in a window air-conditioner in the summertime.

While they showed her the room, Oriana learned that Mrs. Neville had been born in this very house and Mr. Neville was the son of a minister. Mr. Neville had intended to become a minister to, or a lawyer, or possibly an architect, but he'd always been in delicate health and so he'd never gone to college.

The Nevilles had gotten married in the early part of 1929 and they'd gone to Europe for their honeymoon. They'd planned to spend a year there, but they'd had to come back because of the market crash, you know. And they'd had to take care of her father until the day he died because he'd become an invalid and would just sit and stare straight ahead. They'd always been afraid that he might shoot himself or jump out of a window like some of those Wall Street stockbrokers, but he had lived on for another twenty-three years.

In 1930, they'd had to begin renting rooms, but they didn't really mind because both of them liked people and they'd never been able to have children.

Oriana had kitchen privileges, Mrs. Neville had said, and her kitchen was just down the hall. It had once been the kitchen for the butler and his wife, but now she'd have to share it with four other people, but they were all nice and there'd never been any trouble.

And the Nevilles rented mostly to students from the business and vocational schools in the neighborhood, but sometimes they had college students as well. The university was just half a mile away. But they really preferred the vocational and business students, you know, because they were so much more adult and serious. They didn't seem to have time for pranks like college students.

And the Nevilles had their own quarters downstairs on the first floor just off the entrance hall. It use to be a dining room but they had converted it into a living-bedroom combination and really that was all the space they needed. The big double doors were always open and you could drop in for a chat any time you wanted to.

Oriana found that the Nevilles were very seldom alone. There had almost always been someone with them having tea and cookies.

But occasionally, when Oriana had returned from her classes, she might find just Mr. or Mrs. Neville sitting beyond their open doors.

He would be in his easy chair holding what always seemed to be the same book and when he saw Oriana, he would close the book and smile, and Mrs. Neville would invite her in.

Mr. Neville was quite a scholar, Mrs. Neville told Oriana, even though he hadn't been to college, and he could read Latin and Greek. And even do calculus. And he hadn't been out of the house for the past thirty years, even to the front porch, because even a slight breeze could be dangerous to his constitution.

Every December, the Nevilles sent Christmas cards to everyone who had ever spent any time in their house, if they knew their addresses now and last year's card hadn't been returned address unknown or sometimes even deceased. Almost four hundred cards. And they got stacks and stacks of cards themselves. Really, so many. Mrs. Neville pinned them to the drapes, from ceiling to floor, and Scotch taped the rest to the walls on both sides of the fireplace.

Oriana received the news that Deveraux place had been bought up by a Savannah bank and so she had been able to go to school full time. She would make her breakfast in the third floor kitchen and get to school for the eight-thirty class and be back around four-thirty. After supper she would turn on the radio to someone talking so that she could practice her shorthand for a while and then she would turn to music and read until it was time to go to bed.

When Oriana graduated from the yearlong course, she had half a dozen job offers--all of the graduates usually did--and she had more or less at random chosen to work for Fergusson Construction. It was just a typing job for now, the recruiting lady had explained, but the Fergusson company was a big firm and there were lots of opportunities for promotion. All of the new girls started in the typing pool, but as soon as there were openings, they would move up.

Oriana had kept her room at the Nevilles, even though it meant a thirty minute bus ride and two transfers.

She had been in the typing pool two months when she had seen Mike for the first time. She hadn't known who he was at the time, of course. She had never seen the president of the company and she didn't even know his name, or care.

But she had known that he must be somebody important from the way Mrs. Jarris, the head of the typing pool, jumped up from her desk and rushed over to see what he wanted.

He had stood there, looking at the girls, and then he had said something to Mrs. Jarris and left.

Mrs. Jarris had come to Oriana's desk and told her that she was to go up to the president's office because he wanted a girl to do some typing for him. And Gretchen, who had the desk next to hers, had grinned. "Have a good time, dearie."

Oriana had gone up to Mike's office and he had handed her some second sheets and asked her to make copies. She had asked how many and he said that two or three of each would be enough. They had been letters to a company in Buffalo and the correspondence had been almost a year old.

Oriana had begun typing and Mike sat down at his desk. He had riffled through some papers and he had seemed impatient. After a short while, he had gotten up abruptly and walked over to her typewriter. He had stood behind her watching, and then he had put his fingertips on her shoulders and begun talking.

Oriana had stopped typing. She had felt cold, remembering the last time someone had touched her.

Mike had said that all this work was really a bore, wasn't it, and why didn't they go out and have lunch. It was almost that time anyway. Maybe a few drinks after and he knew of a quiet place. Maybe they wouldn't come back to the office at all today.

Oriana had looked up and said no. He had stared at her, his face flushing, and then said, "The hell with the typing. Get out of here."

She had gone back downstairs and when she sat down at her desk, Gretchen had said, "My, that was quick."

I'm going to get fired now, Oriana had thought. He's going to phone Mrs. Jarris and I'm going to get fired and have to start looking for another job.

The phone on Mrs. Jarris' desk had rung and Mrs. Jarris had sat almost at attention as she listened. Then she had nodded and hung up. She had gone to Gretchen, spoken to her, and then gone back to her desk.

Gretchen had picked up her purse and winked at Oriana. "You had your chance, honey. I know he likes my typing."

Mrs. Jarris had brought Oriana some work to do and Oriana had been surprised. "I'm not fired?"

"No, dear," Mrs. Jarris had said gently. "You're not fired."

The next day Mrs. Jarris had come to her desk again. "Mr. Hegan would like to see you in his office."

Oriana had shaken her head. "I'm not going."

Mrs. Jarris had regarded her curiously. "Mr. Hegan said that he wanted to apologize for anything out of line he might have said the last time." Then she had sighed. "Oriana, I'm not telling you that it means my job if you don't go up there, because it really doesn't. But as a favor to yourself, why not go up there and at least listen? Who knows, you might hear something good. You can always walk out again if you don't like what you hear."

Oriana had been reluctant, but she had gone up to Mike's office and this time he had left the door open. He had begun to apologize immediately. He said that he felt really sorry about anything he might have said that offended her the last time. But he'd been drinking. Though he didn't drink often. He'd had business worries and he had just forgotten himself. He promised that nothing like that would ever happen again.

He told her that his private secretary--that gray-haired lady out there at the electric typewriter--was retiring soon and he needed a replacement. The job he was offering Oriana paid more than twice what she earned in the typing pool. And she had been recommended because she was a hard and loyal worker. The job carried responsibilities that required intelligence and he was sure that she could handle it.

She had listened and watched him and not really believed what he said. But she thought she had also seen something else. He wasn't ever going to touch her again unless she let him. And she wasn't going to let.

"All right," she had said. "I'll try."

There really hadn't been too much for her to learn. Mike seemed to have delegated most of the work to others and he just made a decision now and then and Oriana suspected that it was always the decision that his people expected of him. So there had been time for Mike to talk and she had learned about Laurie and Henry and Eve until she had almost felt that she knew them personally.

Mike had asked her about herself, but she had told him as little as possible. However, one morning she had found herself talking--remembering some of the good things about the island. She hadn't been aware of how long she talked, but suddenly she had realized what she was doing and stopped.

A few weeks went by and then Mike had come to the office one morning and said, "I've been thinking about this island of yours, Oriana. I'm going down there and have a look at it myself."

She had been surprised, of course. "But why?"

"Business, Oriana. Business. I've got some big ideas about islands and how to turn a buck. Why not come with me and show me around?"

Oriana had never planned on returning to the island again. It was the buried past. And yet....

Mike had smiled quickly. "I'll get us seats on opposite sides of the plane and separate accommodations wherever we stay. This is no proposition. And I can produce a half dozen character references, if you want them."

They had flown down to Savannah and hired a boat to take them to the island.

They had landed at the Deveraux jetty and she had found the house almost the same as it had been the day she left--just a little older and the roofline sagging a little more. Her mother's bedroom and the kitchen could still be lived in and there were still full brandy bottles in the cellar.

She had wanted to walk farther inland, all the way to the ruins of the Forrest plantation. She had wanted to stand there, just dreaming, as she had done so often after Pitts left the island. But she would have wanted to do that alone and so she hadn't even suggested that they go on to the Forrest place.

When they walked back to the boat, Mike had said, "The Deveraux house must have been a real beauty when you were a little girl."

It hadn't been, of course, but she had just nodded.

They returned to the mainland where Mike had them registered in one of Savannah's finest hotels and then he had left her saying that he had some business in town.

Oriana hadn't seen him again until toward the evening of the next day when he pressed the buzzer at her door.

He had been smiling, almost grinning, and she could tell that he'd been drinking, but he had stayed out in the hall. "Oriana, we're going out tonight and celebrate."

"Celebrate?"

"I'll tell you all about it at dinner."

He had taken her to a restaurant and when they sat down, he had asked her if she would like a drink while they waited for their dinner.

She had said no, but he had ordered for himself. A double scotch.

He had begun talking. "I've been running around from one place to another. It turns out that a bank here owns half of the island. The other half is in the name of some-body named Forrest. I got the impression that the bank thinks of the property as a white elephant, so people were ready to listen when I made an offer. Oriana, I bought the Deveraux house."

Oriana had stared at him and waited.

"I guess the island got under my skin, Oriana. Even if I've seen it just once. I'm going to restore the Deveraux house. Your home. And when I'm finished, it will look just like it did the first day anybody moved in. Better. And I've got options to buy more land. As much as I want. Maybe some day I'll even pick up Forrest's half."

His drink had come. "Why can't that island be a big thing again, Oriana? I don't mean cotton or rice. I mean big homes, golf courses, marinas. All it needs is a little promotion and it could mean big money."

Oriana had listened to him talk and thought maybe he really is going to do all of those things to the island, but that isn't why he bought the house I was born in. That isn't why he's going to spend a lot of money restoring it to what he thinks it was when I lived here. Oriana had felt a little sad because now she ralized how much he wanted to please her. But there had been something else too. Now she could see something beyond the Deveraux house. And it changed everything.

After dinner they had gone back to the hotel and when Mike had lingered at the door, waiting and telling her again how beautiful the Deveraux house would be once more, she had asked him to come in for a drink.

She had called room service and ordered a bottle of scotch, a bottle of brandy, soda and ice.

When they were brought up, she had poured herself a small glass of brandy at first because she had never tasted brandy before and she didn't know what to expect.

Later that night, after Mike had fallen asleep beside her, she had gotten up and taken a long shower.

Then she had sat down in an easy chair and begun dreaming about the island.

It would take a lot of money to rebuild the Forrest place. A lot, lot more than restoring the Deveraux house.

And why couldn't it be built again? There must be plans somewhere. Perhaps in some dusty courthouse office. And she remembered all of the things that belonged inside--the furniture, the chandeliers, the mirrors, every single piece. It would take a lot of money. A lot.

She had looked at Mike sleeping. No, it would be too

much to ask that of him now. Nothing that grand. But she would wait and the time would come. Let him re-build the Deveraux place first.

When they returned north, she had moved to an apart-ment closer to the company offices. Mike had wanted to buy her a fur coat, but she had said no. The idea of wear-ing one made her uneasy. Maybe it was just because she had come from the South where you didn't see those things too often. Or maybe it just seemed too much of a symbol of what she had become.

Mike had expected her to quit her job, but she had in-sisted upon keeping it. She felt better doing something useful instead of just waiting in an apartment.

And then one day Laurie walked into the office.

Mike had been somewhere else in the building and Or-iana had been alone. She had never seen Laurie before, of course, except in photographs.

It had been awkward. Oriana just hadn't known what to do or say. And she had wondered why Laurie was there.

Laurie had studied her. "So Mike is going to buy him-self an island?"

"Yes," Oriana had said. "I think so."

"The place where you were born and raised?"

Oriana had felt herself coloring. "Yes."

Laurie had smiled. Somehow it had been a nice smile and Oriana had thought, why have I done this to her.

"You're a pretty girl," Laurie had said. "Nice white skin and that really black hair. Not at all like me. I'm all pink and blonde. Sometimes I'd like to try something else."

Laurie had glanced at some papers on Mike's desk. "Mike's been relaxed and happy the last few weeks and I like to see him happy. As a matter of fact I like to see ev-erybody happy. Have you met Eve?"

"Yes. I see her almost every day."

Laurie had nodded. "That's right, I forgot. She works here. Well, then you ought to know something about her. But maybe not much. Eve is a world to herself."

Mike had come into the office and when he saw Laurie, he had hesitated, not knowing what might have happened or what might have been said.

Laurie had smiled. "I was in the neighborhood shopping and I thought I'd drop by and snoop. I like your secretary, Mike. A nice girl. Why don't we invite her over to the house for the weekend?"

Oriana had wanted to say no, I couldn't possibly do anything like that, but Laurie had just gone on. "We can talk a little. No arguments now. I'll be expecting you."

When Laurie was gone, Mike had said, "What happened here?"

"Nothing really. Mike, I can't spend the weekend at your house. It just wouldn't be right."

Mike had thought about it and shrugged. "Don't worry about it. Everything will be all right."

At the end of that week, Mike had picked her up at her apartment and they had driven on to Mike's house.

It was located in one of the hilly suburbs and they had been stopped at a gate by private security guards before they were allowed to enter the area. Once inside, their car followed a long winding asphalt road. Through the trees, here and there, Oriana could glimpse the roofs of large mansions. At last they turned into a driveway that ended in an oval before a huge French Provincial.

At dinner, both Henry and Eve had watched her curiously and silently and Oriana had felt quite uneasy wondering what they were thinking and if they knew anything.

But gradually, during the rest of the evening, Oriana had relaxed, because Laurie had done most of the talking and she could make you feel at ease.

Oriana had gone up to bed at about eleven. She had been nearly asleep when she had heard the soft knocking at her door.

Her first thought had been, God, I don't have any brandy up here. Then she had gone to the door and put her hand on the knob, but she knew that she couldn't open it. She had whispered. "Not here, Mike. I couldn't. Not in this house."

She had heard low laughter from the other side of the

door. Laurie.

Oriana had closed her eyes and she had heard Laurie say, "It's all right, Oriana. Open the door. I won't bite."

Oriana had opened the door, feeling embarrassed and ashamed.

Laurie had smiled. "That's what I was going to tell you, Oriana, but you took the words right out of my mouth. You and Mike can do it anywhere, but not under this roof. I think I should draw the line there or God will think I don't care."

Oriana's face had turned crimson. "You know about us, but still you invited me here?"

"I wanted a closer, longer look. I'd like to find out what kind of a person you are. I've got my reasons."

"How did you find out about us?"

"I've been expecting something like this and when I heard that Mike had got himself a new young secretary, I thought bingo."

Oriana had looked away. "I'll leave."

"Hell, no. Stick around. I thought I'd tell you everything's okay because I didn't want you to go around feeling guilty and thinking that you stabbed me in the back or something. Relax, Oriana. Everything's going to turn out just fine."

"I just don't understand this."

Laurie had smiled again. "Good night, now. Sleep tight."

Oriana had been invited to stay the next weekend and the next and soon it was rare for her not to be there from Friday evening until Monday morning.

On week days, she would go back to her apartment after work. Sometimes Mike would take her out to dinner and sometimes not. But if he didn't show up by nine o'clock, she knew she could put the brandy bottle away.

fourteen

How long had Clara been in there? Sixteen hours? At least that. Certainly that should be enough.

But still he approached the freezer cautiously. He put his ear to its side and listened. Nothing. He tapped its side, half-panicked at the thought that he might hear a knock in return.

Silence.

He began taking the cases of brandy off the freezer lid.

Yes, Clara was quite dead. And frozen. But she hadn't gone easily. Her fingers were raw and bloodied with the struggle, and the two wire baskets inside were bent and mangled. Her open dead eyes stared up at him and Bowler was now thankful that he had drunk as much brandy as he had.

He would have to get rid of the body.

No one could possibly believe that Clara had taken refuge in the freezer to avoid the tiger and that somehow it had locked, turned itself on, and she had frozen to death.

Bowler wiped his forehead with a handkerchief. He would drag Clara's body outside and leave it in the underbrush where the tiger was bound to find it when the rain stopped.

Did tigers eat dead things? Things they hadn't killed themselves? He didn't know. Some predators didn't. But he hoped that tigers did. He fervently hoped so.

He would tell people that Clara had been sicker than he had thought, and feverish. She must have been in a delirium. During the night she must have risen from her bed, dressed, and wandered outside. And the tiger had gotten her.

But how would he get the body out of the cellar? Clara outweighed him by at least thirty pounds and he was not particularly strong. Should he let her thaw out first? Good Heavens, no. She would be dead weight and simply flop all over. It would just make matters worsse.

No. He would leave her frozen. She ought to be easier to handle that way. She would be stiff. He could utilize leverage to get her out of the freezer. Yes.

But leverage or not, it proved to be a desperate job getting Clara out of there and onto the floor.

He paused to rest. What now? It was obviously out of the question for him to even attempt carrying her. She would somehow have to be dragged. He searched the cellar until he came upon a coil of rope.

He returned to Clara's body. Should he put a loop of the rope around her neck? No, that wouldn't do at all. It might leave burn marks. If the tiger didn't eat that part of Clara, people would certainly ask questions. The ankles? No. Somehow that seemed, well, just a bit undignified and possibly even obscene.

He remembered the tarpaulin he'd seen in his search for the rope and fetched it. Yes, this would do nicely. The canvas even had grommets through which he could fasten the rope. He rolled Clara onto the tarpaulin, folded it around her. and ran the rope several times around her body.

He opened the cellar door to the outside world. It was still raining steadily. Good.

It was quite a job pulling Clara over the cellar floor and outside. Once he got onto the wet turf, there seemed to be considerabley less friction, but this presented him with another problem. Traction. He simply wasn't getting enough traction with his smooth-soled shoes. He kept slipping and falling.

He sighed. There was nothing to do but remove his shoes and even his socks. Clara had often made it a practice to go barefoot when they were alone in the kitchen. It had always grated him, the sight and sound of large bare feet scraping over linoleum and wood.

He removed his shoes and socks and placed them

aside on the wet grass. He tested his bare toes on the cool turf. Ah, that felt rather good at that. He giggled. Perhaps there was something to be said for an occasional reversion to the primitive.

Pulling Clara became easier now, though still laboriously slow. He would leave Clara somewhere past the slave cabins where the tiger was bound to find her tomorrow when the rain stopped. It did seem to be attracted to the house and grounds.

The wind rose and keened and robbed breath from his lungs. Sudden gusts nearly forced him to his knees but he pushed doggedly on, digging his toes into the earth.

After what seemed ages, he finally reached the last of the slave cabins. This was really far enough. He dragged Clara's body behind the building, in the lee of the wind. Even the lashing rain slanted almost horizontally just overhead without touching him.

He crouched down and began untying his bundle.

Yes, it was rather nice down near the ground. Like a warm cave. A cozy nest.

He listened to his own heavy breathing. And then he heard the breathing of something else.

He turned and stared into the face of the tiger.

fifteen

In the morning the rain stopped and gray-white fog pulled in from the sea.

Laurie and Oriana prepared and served breakfast.

"The Bowlers are gone," Laurie said. "Just disappeared. Where they went and why, I don't know."

Henry helped himself generously to scrambled eggs. "Probably they thought there was some safer place on the island. But I wonder why Bowler took off his shoes and socks."

They waited.

"His shoes and socks," Henry said. "Or at least I think they're his shoes and socks. They're outside just at the beginning of the back garden. You can't see them from here because of the fog. I left them there so if Bowler comes back he'll find them waiting."

Laurie frowned. "Henry, have you been outside again?" He nodded. "I took another note to the dock. I thought the old one would be blown away during the night and I was right. I put the new note in a picture frame. With glass in front, you know. It's sort of waterproof and I tied it to one of the pilings." Henry looked toward the windows. "But if this fog doesn't let up, I don't think we're going to see Mike today either."

"Where's MacIntyre?" Laurie asked. "Is he still sick?"

"He is not sick," Henry said. "At least not in the usual sense. He's in his bathroom with the door locked. Bathrooms are the safest places in the house because they have doors that tigers can't see through and know you're there."

After they finished breakfast, Laurie took a tray upstairs.

In the living room, Eve reached into her knitting bag and brought out needles and yarn.

Henry watched her. "I never saw you knit before."

"I never have, Henry, but I thought I'd give it a try. This seems to be the right time for this sort of thing. When we're just waiting."

"Is that one of Laurie's knitting bags?"

"Yes, Henry."

"What are you knitting?"

"Really nothing in particular, Henry. Just practicing. Why are you so interested?"

"I don't know. It's just that I could never picture you knitting before."

Laurie rejoined them. She held one hand behind her back. "Guess what I found."

She brought the hand into view and opened it. "A genuine rifle cartridge. I thought I'd go through Mike's jackets in the closet just on the off-chance and I hit pay dirt."

Forrest examined the cartridge. "I don't suppose you found any more like this?"

"No. That's it. One of Mike's jackets has a pocket with a hole and the bullet slipped into the lining. So now you can shoot our tiger. I suppose there really is one?"

Forrest smiled. "You don't think that there is a tiger?"

Laurie shrugged. "Just about everybody's seen the tiger except me. Maybe it's like UFOs. Some people see them and some people don't. I guess I'm not a tiger person."

Henry had left the room and he now returned with Mike's Weatherby. He handed the rifle to Forrest. "I think you'd better do the shooting. I suppose you're going out and track down the tiger?"

"No, Henry. Not with just one bullet. We use it only if we have to. Only if the tiger comes back."

Henry nodded. "I think the best thing for us to do is to use the second floor rear veranda as a sort of observation post. I mean the only place the tiger's been seen is out there. If he comes back, we can see him easier because we're occupying higher ground. Or at least higher veranda."

Forrest slipped the cartridge into the Weatherby and snapped on the safety. "It's a big island, Henry. The tiger may never show up here again."

"Maybe not. But I think he's near." Henry pointed to the dog shivering at Laurie's heel. "He smells the tiger and that means he must be fairly close. Maybe even watching the house, waiting for someone to come out."

Forrest regarded the dog. "I'm going to take Henry's advice and go upstairs where I've got a good view of the back grounds."

Forrest found Henry following him up the stairs to the second floor veranda. Forrest sat down in a wicker chair facing the garden and Henry took the chair beside him.

A breeze came up and the fog began slowly lifting. After a while Forrest thought he could make out Bowler's shoes and socks.

"Animals are curious," Henry said. "All animals. That's because the lives they lead are really boring. Even to them. So they're curious about anything new because it breaks the monotony. If you go into the woods and sit down and are real quiet, after about fifteen minutes all kinds of animals you never suspected were even there will come out of hiding to get a look at you. The secret is not to move or make noises."

Henry was silent for a while and then said, "Basically you're a spectator, aren't you?"

"Spectator, Henry?"

"Yes. A spectator. A watcher. What I mean is that all of your life you've just watched other people living. You never really participated. You've never had to ask for help or give any."

"Are you asking for help, Henry?"

"No. It's too late for that. I'm too old. The tree is bent."

Yes, Forrest thought, maybe Henry's right. A spectator. A watcher. Like my father. He was a watcher. Always patiently in the background at those endless parties Mother gave. Standing somewhere near the wall, smiling politely, and wondering when it would all be over.

His father hadn't even told anyone when he learned how sick he was. He hadn't wanted to bother people. Not his wife. Not his son. He had just quietly come back down here. The Forrest house had been gone, of course, but he had rented a small cottage on the mainland and waited to die. When it had happened, he had been buried in the family plot on the island. The family lawyer had sent them letters telling them what had happened--Forrest at his school in Switzerland and his mother in London. She was in Rome now, with her third husband.

Henry leaned forward. "I see the tiger. He's been there all the time. Watching us. He moved just a little and movement gives you away."

"Where, Henry?"

"He blends in with things, but if you just stare at the grass at the foot of the first oak, after a while you'll be able to make him out."

Forrest studied the spot for nearly a minute before he was certain. "Yes, I see him now." Forrest slowly brought the rifle up until it rested on the veranda railing.

"Are you going to shoot him?"

"I think I should, Henry. We can't have a tiger roaming loose on the island, can we?" Henry nodded. "You'll have to shoot him, if for no other reason than that he killed Pitts. When animals kill humans they have to be killed in return. That's the rule. Are you going to shoot him while he's just lying there? I mean don't you want to make it sporting and wait until he charges?"

"Henry, there are times when you can afford to be sporting and times when you don't dare to be. Especially when you've got a .300 rifle and just one cartridge."

Henry agreed. "If we were all members of a tiger hunting party with plenty of bullets and voluntarily risking our lives, then we'd practically have to be sporting. But that isn't the case here. We're protecting ourselves and that gives us the right to shoot any time we want to. Besides, I don't think the tiger will charge. He looks content where he is."

Forrest centered the sights of the rifle's scope on a point just behind the tiger's shoulder blade. He exhaled slowly and squeezed the trigger.

The tiger leaped to its feet and then dropped to the ground, twitching convulsively.

Henry went to the veranda railing. "He's dead, all right. Completely dead. Notice how fat and stuffed his belly looks? I wonder what's in there." Henry smiled. "I'll tell MacIntyre that it's safe to come out of the bathroom now."

sixteen

It was nice to be able to leave the French doors open again and let in fresh air.

Laurie glanced up at the moon and then returned to her dressing table.

Why the hell wasn't Mike back yet? The rain had stopped early in the morning and the fog had gone away. The afternoon had been perfect. What was keeping him on the mainland?

She brushed some face powder off the surface of the dressing table and admired the glass. Really a swell piece of furniture. Custom made and a lot more expensive than the kind Jacobi sold. Even now.

When Laurie had learned that Mike had gotten married, she had begun dating Albert Jacobi and it wasn't long before he asked her to marry him, which she had been expecting, of course. She had thought about it before, and already decided, well, why not? Al's not a bad guy. I could do a lot worse.

It had been a big wedding and reception. They had rented the Turnerverein Hall and there had been plenty to eat and drink. A four-piece band played from eight in the evening until past one in the morning when union rules said they had to quit. Over five hundred people had showed up, not counting kids, and the whole thing was a big success.

Albert's father owned the second-hand furniture store on Vine Street and he made Albert a full partner as a wedding present. It was a good business and could support two families, but Albert liked to get ahead and so he talked his father into opening another store on the South Side with himself in charge.

Albert was the kind of person who lived the furniture business from morning to night and he would get restless on Sundays when the store was closed. So things went good and the upshot of it was that today there were six Jacobi furniture stores in the city and five of them sold new furniture only.

She didn't see Mike for nearly three years and then one day he turned up and said that he had just happened to be going through the neighborhood and he thought he'd drop in and look up a few old friends.

He took her out to dinner and towards the end of the evening he had mentioned why couldn't they go to a hotel, but she had told him that she was a married woman now and maybe it was old fashioned, but she respected her marriage vows and would be true to them. So they had parted just friends and she didn't see Mike again for seven or eight years.

Laurie and Albert were married six years and still no kids, so she had gone to this doctor out of the neighborhood and found out that she couldn't have any. You could have knocked her over with a feather. It was just about the last thing she had ever expected, and she had only gone to the doctor because she wanted to break the ice so that Albert would go to see him too and get himself checked out.

She didn't go into any depression or anything like that. Mainly she was just surprised. Albert was the one who took it really hard. Both him and his old man. They thought that this was the end of the Jacobi family line because Albert was an only child.

So Laurie had said why the hell can't we adopt a kid or two, but Albert said that it wasn't really the same. Not like a real blood line.

Nearly two years went by and then Albert had brought up the adoption thing again himself. Laurie had said okay and let's get on some waiting lists, but Albert had said what do you know, I just happen to know a single woman who has a year-old boy that she can't afford to keep and maybe I could persuade her to give the kid up.

It turned out that this single woman with the kid was Annie Gardner, whom Laurie remembered from high school.

When Laurie got a look at the kid, she could tell that he was going to grow up looking a lot like Albert. And she could see that Annie wasn't all that crazy about giving up the boy, so she had wondered how much money had changed hands.

Laurie had thought the situation over. Annie was a good clean kid and somehow she felt sorry for her, and Albert too. So Laurie had just come right out with it and told them that wouldn't it be simpler if they all faced the facts and if she got a divorce without hard feelings and Albert could marry Annie.

They had all parted on good terms with Annie crying and Albert too. Laurie got the divorce and Albert was nice and generous with a settlement.

He married Annie as soon as he was eligible and today they had three boys and they still exchanged Christmas cards.

So after the divorce, Laurie was free and independent for about three months when Mike looked her up again and said he'd heard about the divorce.

They went out to dinner and he told her that he was doing real well for himself. He was president of the company now because Myra's father had got himself killed when his plane had crashed while he was going up to his Canadian fishing lodge.

She had asked him how Myra was and his son Henry, and Mike said all right, but he didn't talk anymore about them.

They had spent the night in her apartment and in the morning Mike flew back home. He phoned her the next day and said he'd found a nice apartment for her out there. She had thought about it for a couple of days because she hated to leave the neighborhood where she knew everybody, but finally decided to go anyway.

The apartment had been really terrific. It had this view of hundreds of tall buildings which were especially beautiful at night. When Mike told her how much he was paying rent, she had almost fainted. But it looked like he could afford it and he let her have a pretty free hand when it came to buying clothes.

It had all been exciting, but lonely too. There was hardly anybody she could talk to except Mike and he came once a week or sometimes twice. She was beginning to think about going back home, when Myra drowned. Nobody knew exactly how it happened, but it was at that Canadian fishing lodge. It looked like she had gone out onto the dock to look at the water or something and somehow she had just slipped off and drowned. They had found her body at the end of the dock in the morning.

When she saw Mike after the funeral, she had told him that she was thinking of going back home. But Mike had said why didn't they just get married--after a decent interval?

So that was what happened and she moved into Mike's big house. There were servants and she got to meet the people Mike invited over and got invited in return and always had a good time. Nobody was what you might call high society, but they were all in the contracting business or trucking or unions and nobody, including their wives, was at all high hat.

When Laurie married Mike, Henry came with the deal, of course. He was a quiet kid with glasses and he took after his mother in looks. He hardly ever said a word. Not that he resented her or anything like that. Actually he seemed to like her, but she couldn't put her arms around him. You could see that he was uncomfortable when anybody tried it. He just liked to be let alone, but at the same time he liked to be with her. Just in the same room, maybe in a corner reading. And when she moved to another room because she had something to do there, he would follow and go on reading.

It was hard for her to understand him because she had come from a family that was all the time hugging and kissing. So she had settled for mussing Henry's hair about once a week. It would make him blush, but she could see he liked it if it didn't happen too often.

Henry and Mike got along okay, but they were never close. To tell the truth, Mike just didn't seem interested in the kid at all. He hardly even noticed when Henry graduated from high school almost valedictorian and Laurie had been the only one who attended the ceremony.

Henry always got good grades in school and you'd think that he'd be satisfied just being an egghead, but he was always trying something physical, like body building and lifting weights, but it never made any difference that she could see. Maybe he got stronger, but it didn't show. He still stayed skinny and he never did grow to be tall.

Henry had even tried out for the football team, but got bumped before picture day, so he had nothing to show for it. He would do a lot of running too. He'd get up early in the morning, even before daylight sometimes, and he would run for hours, but he never got fast enough to make the track team either. He seemed to try everything that came along and finally he hooked into swimming. It seemed like one day he couldn't swim a stroke and the next day swimming was almost his life.

He won all kinds of medals and trophies for swimming long distances. He didn't seem to have much luck in the shorter races. Laurie had gone to his swimming meets in college and there was little Henry and a half dozen others going back and forth, back and forth, from one end of the pool to the other, and eventually Henry would win the race which must have taken twenty minutes or longer.

Laurie stopped brushing her hair and looked down at Willie.

The small dog stood stiff-legged, shivering. He faced the open French doors.

Laurie patted his head. "What's wrong, Willie? Something making you nervous? Just settle down somewhere and take it easy."

Laurie pried the snap cap off a small bottle and shook out two capsules. She washed them down with a half glass of water.

How old had Eve been when Mike took her in?

Thirteen? Yes, about that, but you got the feeling that Eve was older than that when you saw her. Not because of her build, because there wasn't much there at the time. Not like Laurie had been at the same age. It was something in Eve's eyes that made her older.

When Mike announced that he wanted to adopt Eve, it had come right out of the blue.

"Why?" Laurie had asked. She had been thinking about Albert Jacobi and how he had managed to come up with a kid.

Mike had told her that Eve's stepfather was a widower who had just been killed in a accident at one of the gravel pits. "The kid's all alone in the world. No relatives at all. She'll be sent to an orphanage if we don't do anything."

Laurie hadn't been hard-hearted, she had just wanted to know. "So? I mean what is this kid to you personally?"

"I guess I just feel guilty about him getting killed while working for the company. And now his kid is going to be shipped away to some institution."

Of course Laurie hadn't believed that. About Mike feeling guilty. That just wasn't his style.

"She won't be a bother," Mike had said. "Not like a baby or a little kid. She's thirteen. She's been keeping house for her stepfather for years. She'll be spending most of her time in school and doing homework and things like that."

So Laurie had thought, well, why not? Having only one kid in a family is either a mistake or a hobby. Maybe Henry needed a sister and maybe they were already related by blood.

Laurie remembered the first time Eve had set foot in the house. She had just stood there in the foyer and her eyes had gone over everything and it was a while before she took another step into the room.

Laurie had studied the kid and she still hadn't been able to figure it out. For one thing, Eve didn't look like Mike in any way. Laurie was good at spotting things like that and there just wasn't a bit of Mike in her at all. Laurie had begun to wonder if Mike really did feel guilty about the kid's stepfather dying.

Henry had been seventeen when Eve came into the house. Four years older than Eve. So Laurie had got to thinking, hell, if you read the marriage license columns in the newspapers you see a lot of people getting married who already have the same address. That was nature for

122

you and why not? After all, Henry was going to need someone strong who could point him in the right direction and she could see that Eve was a strong person. Even at thirteen.

Laurie had bided her time and Eve and Henry had gotten along fine. No arguing or fighting. Neither one of them was the type for that, when you got right down to it. On the other hand, they never seemed to get particularly close either.

After Eve passed her sixteenth birthday, Laurie would sort of remind them both that they weren't related by blood and she would leave the house afternoons and say that she positively wouldn't be back for three or four hours, but as far as she knew they never even touched each other.

Laurie finished brushing her hair. She made herslf a mixed drink and moved to the chaise lounge.

Willie whimpered, his eyes still fixed on the open veranda doors.

"What's wrong with you?" Laurie asked.

She sipped from her glass. It was funny how life went but there was no use complaining. You never knew what was going to happen next. When you got right down to it, nobody did.

Willie began to growl. He backed up until he was at Laurie's feet.

The tiger moved into the open doorway and stared at Laurie.

Laurie slowly put down her glass. She could feel her heart beating. Beating hard.

Lord, she thought, this is it. This is finally it.

The dog began barking.

seventeen

Mike woke and glanced at his watch. Nearly midnight. Hell, he'd been away almost forty-eight hours.

He wondered what they were thinking about him back there on the island.

He sighed.

Mike had learned early that old man Fergusson did a lot of whoring around. There was always something on the line.

Mike wouldn't have minded something extra himself, but Fergusson had an eye on him and if Mike had tried anything like that, the hypocritical bastard would probably have kicked him out on his can.

So Mike had stayed away from other women, but it had been rough. And Myra just didn't make up for what he was missing.

He'd begun thinking about Laurie and he'd even been tempted to go back and make some kind of an arrangement, but there had been just too much at stake to risk having the old man find out.

So he'd waited until the old man died before he saw Laurie again.

Now Laurie was the kind of a woman a man wanted around. She never hung onto you like a leech. She took you as you were and let you be free.

He remembered the old loft.

He'd fixed it up with a mattress, pillows, blankets and a radio. But it could get cold up there in the winter and hot in summer. He'd had to open that trap door to get some ventilation.

And there would be old Jamie, hiding in that tree, thinking that nobody knew he was there. He'd be watching what happened, his eyes bugging, his tongue hanging out.

The first time Mike had noticed him up there, he'd wanted to jump up and knock Jamie off the tree. But Mike had been right in the middle of something and he didn't want to stop. And when he was finished and lying there, he had thought, what the hell, maybe Jamie learned something.

When you got right down to it, having Jamie there watching added something to the event. Like an actor and his audience.

So Mike had done nothing at all about Jamie or said anything to Laurie. If she'd known that Jamie had been watching all those times, she would have killed him.

And then one day Jamie wasn't there. Maybe he'd decided he'd learned enough and was going to try it on his own.

Mike had been married to Myra three years when the old man died in the plane crash. Mike had been supposed to go to the fishing lodge with him, but he had begged off saying that he had the flu.

When the old man's plane had reached the lake and tried to land, one of its pontoons had collapsed and both Fergusson and a typist from the company office pool had been killed.

Mike had thought that he would be mentioned in the will and he was. For a lousy hundred thousand dollars. Hell, he and the old man had gotten along better than a hundred thousand dollars.

Myra got everything. Real estate, bonds, cars, the firm, the whole works.

Mike had wondered what would happen to the company once the tax people got through with Fergusson's estate, but the old man had been thinking ahead and he had hired himself good estate planners and when the dust settled, the company was as strong as ever.

Mike had waited about six months before he had let

Myra know that he was unhappy about something. "Myra, when you get right down to it, I'm just hired help at the company."

She had been surprised that he felt that way. "But you're the president of the company."

"That's just a title, Myra. I don't own a damn thing down there."

"But everything I have is ours too."

"I know you mean that, Myra, but I still feel like hired help." He had waited while Myra thought about it.

Then she had said. "You mean you want to have the company in your own name?" She had smiled and nodded. "All right, Mike."

He had stared at her. Just like that? The old man had been right. She was simple. She'd turn everything over to him without any more questions. It had almost made him angry. "Not all of it, of course, Myra. Just enough so that I'd feel like the man in the family."

She had agreed eagerly. "Would eighty percent be enough?"

Mike hadn't remembered ever blushing before. "About fifty-five percent, Myra. That ought to do it."

But it hadn't turned out that easy. Old man Fergusson had been a damn fox. Everything was so tied up by his lawyers that Myra couldn't even give anything away. All she had the power to do was raise Mike's salary as president of the company, and that not more than ten percent a year.

Mike had decided to look up Laurie again. They hadn't exchanged any letters, so he didn't know just what had happened to her in the meantime. When he did locate her, he found that she had married Jacobi.

Mike had talked to Laurie and said that he could fly in every once in a while for a night or two, but Laurie had said no dice. She was married now and she wasn't going to fool around with anybody else period.

Mike had gone away unhappy, but when he heard that Laurie had gotten a divorce, he went back.

This time Laurie listened and he put her up in nice apartment only twenty minutes drive from the company.

126

But Laurie wasn't happy for long. She said she just wasn't the kind of person who liked hiding in an apartment among strangers and getting visited by Mike just once in a while and never knowing when that would be. She'd been all ready to pack up and go back home, but then Myra drowned.

Myra had gotten paler and quieter since her father had died. Had she known about Laurie? No, Mike didn't think so.

He quessed that she looked like that because he just hadn't been spending enough time with her. But when he did, he didn't know what the hell to talk about. To tell the truth, she had begun to get on his nerves, just looking at him like that all the time.

Myra had been found in the water at the foot of the dock at sunrise.

Mike had told the Canadian police that she must have gotten up sometime during the night and wandered out onto the dock to look at the moonlight. She did things like that. And she hadn't paid attention to where she was walking. She must have stepped over the edge of the dock and drowned. She couldn't swim a stroke.

They had asked if she had been moody lately and he had said no. She had been bright and cheerful.

The troopers had asked how Myra and Mike got along. Mike had said fine, just fine. They had never had one argument in their whole married life, and that was true enough. Henry had been about ten or twelve or something and listening. The troopers had asked him questions too and he had backed up everything Mike had said.

When they got back home, Mike had bought Henry a bicycle. It wasn't until he gave it to the kid that he remembered that Henry already had three or four other bikes.

Mike had gone to Laurie and told her that he could marry her now. Laurie had let him know that she couldn't have any more children and he had told her that it didn't matter. What did he want with more kids anyway? Henry was enough.

So after six months Laurie and Mike had gotten married and things rolled along just fine for years and then

Laurie had to go to a doctor because she wasn't feeling just right and she had learned about her heart.

If only she'd kept her damn mouth shut and not told Mike anything. But knowing about her heart and what could happen any second, did something.

Laurie had talked to him about it one night when he'd gotten out of bed and made himself a stiff drink.

She had slipped back into her nightgown. "What's wrong, Mike? I mean what causes it?"

"I don't know. Business worries, I guess."

"You never worried about business before. It's my heart, isn't it? You expect me to drop dead right in the middle of something?"

"Hell, it could happen."

Yes, that had been it. It could happen at any time. He couldn't get that out of his mind. It could happen right there in bed and he'd be looking down at a staring corpse.

Laurie had shrugged. "The doctor told me I could still keep doing it. He said it might even be good for me."

"What the hell does a doctor really know about anything like that? He's not God. He can't guarantee anything."

But after a while, Mike had begun to wonder if the trouble really was Laurie's heart. Could there be more to it than that? Was there something wrong with him now?

He had finally gone down to the company's typing pool. He hadn't been down there more than four or five times a year since he'd married Laurie. She had usually been enough.

He had seen Oriana for the first time.

He had had her sent up to his office and he had shooed away Mrs. Jenson, who had been the old man's secretary and was now his. He had grabbed something from the files and asked Oriana to make copies.

He had let her type for fifteen or twenty minutes while he looked her over. Then he had made the proposition. Hell, it had been stupid of him, but he had thought that she was like the other girls in the pool and knew what to expect.

She had stared at him with those dark eyes, her face expressionless, and said no. Just plain damn no.

He had sent her back downstairs. Who the hell did she think she was anyway. He wasn't used to getting turned down by a damn typist. Maybe she was the kind of a girl who took a little more time, but damn, he didn't have time to fool around for a couple of days. He wanted to know about himself and right now. He had picked up the phone, gotten the typing pool, and had Gretchen sent up. He knew that she wouldn't give him any trouble.

He'd taken Gretchen out to a quick lunch and then to a motel. He'd found out that as far his third leg was concerned, everything was still just fine and dandy.

But that damn typist, Oriana Deveraux, had eaten into him. It was more than that she had hurt his ego. He could get over that. But there was something about her that grabbed him. He didn't know quite what it was, but he knew it was something that could last a long time. Not like it was with girls like Gretchen. Hell, he couldn't even remember what her last name was.

The next day he'd had Oriana sent up again.

The first thing he'd done, of course, had been to apologize for the day before. He said that he'd been drinking and the liquor had gone to his head. He said he just didn't know what had gotten into him and it would never happen again.

He told her that Mrs. Jenson, his secretary, was retiring and that Oriana had been recommended to take her place. He told her that being his private secretary was a great opportunity and would she like the job?

Any other girl would have jumped at that, but she had looked at him and thought it over before she had finally decided that she would give it a try.

Mike had decided that he wasn't going to rush this one. It would take time. He would let her talk about herself and he would listen and there must be some way to get to her.

He and Laurie still slept in the same bedroom, but now in twin beds. Mike hadn't been able to get any decent sleep thinking about waking up one morning and finding someone cold next to him. Every once in a while

Mike would wonder if maybe he should try again, but then he'd decide that he didn't want to go through all that again and go to sleep.

He'd wondered about Laurie. How was she taking having nothing? Especially a woman like Laurie. She was just about made for it. He'd begun to wonder if she really was going without anything at all. Was there somebody who didn't know about her heart, or didn't care?

It had bugged him enough so that he'd hired a private detective. But he came up with nothing. Nothing at all.

One day Mike had come right out with it and asked Laurie how she was able to stand it.

She had said it was like coffee. People think they can't live without coffee and then one day their doctor tells them they got to quit. So they stop drinking coffee and for the first few days, it's hell. But then they start not missing it at all. And after a while they even begin to wonder why people drink coffee in the first place.

Mike hadn't been able to figure out if she was kidding him or not.

In the meantime he'd had to use the girls in the typing pool or he'd stop in at a bar and see what he could pick up.

At the office, he had tried to get Oriana to talk about herself. But she just didn't have much to say. Even to this day, the only thing he knew about her personal life was that she had been born on the island and that she had left it when her mother died.

But when she talked about the island itself or about some of the people who had lived there, he'd seen that dreamy look come into her eyes.

So he had made some excuse to go down there and get a look at the place and he'd taken Oriana with him. He'd found the Deveraux house a mess, everything overgrown or busted. No one could have lived there in the condition the place was then.

But he had watched Oriana from the moment she set foot on the island. It did something to her. This is it, he had thought. This is where she lives. This place where she was born and brought up. This is what put that light into her eyes.

130

Suppose he rebuilt the Deveraux house? Made it look like new. Like it must have been when she lived there?

Yes, that had been the price Hegan had paid for Oriana.

Now he snapped on the night light and got out of bed. He made himself a drink and looked down at Mary Lou.

He decided to wake her.

eighteen

The dog's barking woke Forrest.

He opened his eyes in time to see the tiger bounding past his opened French doors. He froze for moments, sitting upright, then he recovered and slipped quickly out of his bed.

His impulse had been to close and bolt the French doors immediately, but then he realized that he must warn the others first.

He stepped cautiously out onto the rear veranda and saw Henry standing at the rail looking down into the back garden.

Henry pointed. "It disappeared into the brush. But it was up here on the veranda. I was reading in bed and then I heard Willie barking. When I looked up, I saw the tiger running by. I rushed out here, but by then it was gone."

Henry squinted in the direction of the garden again. "I think Willie frightened him away. Do you know why dogs chase cats? Because cats run. Only in this case the dog decided that just barking was enough and you shouldn't expect more than that from just one dog. If there had been a pack, Willie would have followed, but I guess he went back to Laurie's room."

Oriana stepped out onto the veranda. "What in the world is going on? Why was Willie barking like that?"

"Tiger tiger." Henry said.

Oriana stared at them. "Another tiger?"

Eve joined them.

"Another tiger," Henry told her. "But Willie chased it

132

away. It disappeared into the brush and I'll bet it's still running."

Henry frowned. "There's a light in Laurie's room. Maybe she finally saw a tiger. Or maybe she was asleep when Willie started barking. But she should certainly be awake now. Why isn't she out here asking what's going on?"

All of them moved down the veranda and stopped at the open doorway to Laurie's room.

Laurie lay slumped against the back of the chaise lounge, staring at them, unblinking. The dog at her feet whined and looked up at her.

Forrest moved closer. "Laurie?" Henry's face paled. "I think she's dead. The way she's staring and not moving. Her jaw would drop, only the way she's lying prevents it."

Forrest picked up Laurie's limp hand and tried for a pulse.

"It's her heart," Henry said. "She must have seen the tiger. But maybe not. I mean it's possible that her heart might have stopped before the tiger ever got here and he was just a coincidence."

MacIntyre, in a maroon dressing robe, joined them. "What the devil is going on? Why was that fool dog barking? And why is everybody congregated here?" He saw Laurie and blinked. "She's dead," Henry said. "But we don't know for how long. I think we ought to try mouth to mouth resuscitation. CPR, you know?"

MacIntyre stepped closer to Laurie. He touched her face. "CPR wouldn't be any use. She's been dead at least fifteen minutes."

Henry frowned. "How can you tell?"

"I'm a doctor," MacIntyre snapped.

Henry sighed. "Even if we could bring her back now, there'd be severe brain damage. She would be just a vegetable. I don't think anyone of us would want that, would we? We'd better just leave her dead and remember what she was like when she was alive."

MacIntyre turned to Forrest. "Laurie had a diseased heart. We all knew it. This could have happened at any time. Any moment. Perhaps she had a shock of some kind."

Henry smiled faintly. "Don't you know, MacIntyre? There's another tiger loose on the island. Willie's barking chased it away this time, but Forrest and I both saw it."

Fright made its way into MacIntyre's eyes. "Another tiger? How many tigers are there?"

Henry shrugged. "Tiger tiger. When the Chinese mean more than one, they repeat the word. Tiger tiger. But that still doesn't say how many."

MacIntyre's voice became tight. "Where the devil is Mike anyway? Why doesn't he come back and take us off this damn island. He should have come back this afternoon. There was no fog or rain. And it's clear out there right now. He can cross as easily at night as he can in the day time."

"Something might have happened to him," Henry said. "Maybe he didn't get to the mainland at all. The motor conked out and he's just drifting out there on the ocean. Or maybe the boat sank and he drowned. Drowning is terrible, you know. Or maybe he just doesn't want to come back to the island just yet."

"Why wouldn't he want to come back?" MacIntyre demanded.

"I don't know. I just said it was a possibility."

MacIntyre seemed on the verge of panic. "What are we going to do? We can't just wait to be killed by those tigers. Mike may never come back."

Eve reguarded him cooly. "Do you have any suggestions?"

MacIntyre blinked at a thought and then stared at Henry. "Yes, as a matter of fact I have. Why can't Henry swim to the mainland for help? He's swum a lot farther than that before. A lot farther."

"Yes," Henry said softly. "A lot farther."

"I'm surprised you didn't volunteer."

Henry said nothing.

MacIntyre frowned. "Is there some reason you don't want to go for help? Do you want those tigers to kill us all?"

Henry sighed. "All right. If Mike doesn't get back here by morning, I'll go."

MacIntyre persisted. "Why wait until morning? The sooner we get help, the better. Water is water, in the daylight or at night. And you certainly can't get lost. The mainland lights leave a glow on the horizon. All you have to do is swim toward that. It shouldn't take you long to make it over."

Henry smiled faintly. "Suppose the tiger gets me before I even reach the beach? Suppose he's out there right now waiting for me?"

"You can carry a torch of some kind," MaIntyre said. "Animals are afraid of fire."

Henry still retained his smile. "MacIntyre, would you carry the torch and come with me to the beach?"

MacIntyre colored. "There's no need to risk more lives than necessary. Just carry your torch to the water and begin swimming. I don't see any reason why you can't do something like that alone."

Henry looked about. "If nobody comes with me to the beach, how will you know that I'm really swimming to the mainland? I might just hide someplace on the island and wait for the tiger to kill each and every one of you. For my own secret reasons."

"Henry," Oriana said, "if you don't want to swim to the mainland, you don't have to. We'll all be perfectly safe if we just stay inside the house."

Henry thought for several moments. "No, I guess I'll have to give it a try. Now that the subject was brought up. I'll get ready."

After he left the room, Eve bent down and picked up Willie. "There, there," she said. "You'll be all right."

Forrest went down into the back garden, gathered dead twigs and built a small fire. He laid the end of a large branch across the flames.

Henry joined him wearing swimming trunks and sandals and carrying a flashlight.

Forrest pulled the branch from the fire. "I haven't had much experience making torches, Henry. I don't know how well this will work."

"I won't need a torch. Besides, I don't think that one will stay lit. You need to dip it in grease or oil or something that holds a flame in the wind."

The flames flickered and went out. "I've got a flashlight," Henry said. "That's enough so that I don't stumble over anything."

Forrest sighed and tossed the branch back on the fire. "I'll walk with you, Henry."

"You don't have to. I promise I'll go into the water."

"I'm not checking up on you, Henry. I'm just feeling brave and thought you could use the company."

They began walking toward the beach. After a while Henry looked up at the full moon. "Did you know that when you're afraid, nothing is beautiful?"

"Are you worried about the tiger?"

"No, not the tiger. Not at all."

"Henry, call the whole damn thing off."

"No, I can't now. It's like the moment of truth, you know. I have to get everything together."

When they reached the beach, Henry said, "Well, here we are." Good luck, Henry. You'll make it."

Henry handed Forrest the flashlight. He slipped out of his sandals and walked into the water. It reached for his knees, his waist, and then he swam.

Forrest watched until he could no longer see Henry in the moonlight, then he turned and walked back toward the house.

nineteen

He had committed himself.

Henry could feel the pounding of his heart and he had trouble breathing. Easy, he told himself. Easy now.

He rose with the languid movement of the sea and could make out the glow on the western horizon.

He glanced back at the island and the beam of Forrest's flashlight, still so near.

Henry turned back to the open sea, shivering in the cool salt-sticky water. The sea seemed almost asleep. Just the long swell of its heavy breathing. The pale moon seemed to stare down, watching.

There had still been a full moon the night after his mother drowned. Yes, it had been there again.

He had lain on his bunk in the cabin staring at the window and watching the clouds pass over the face of the moon. He hadn't been able to sleep at all.

He had finally slipped out of bed and gone outside. He had been drawn down to the lake shore and out onto the old wooden dock. He had stared down at the dark water a long time, listening to the soft lapping of the wavelets against the pilings.

Had he slipped? Was that what had happened? Had he just slipped? Or had he meant to drop into the black water? He had felt so alone now and life had seemed more than he could possibly bear.

The cold dark water had closed over him. He hadn't struggled. Not at first. He had let his feet sink into the mud and the weeds at the bottom of the lake. It would be just like going to sleep, he had thought. Just darkness and then soft welcome sleep.

But it hadn't been like that at all. Not at all.

There had finally been that demanding gasp for air. That terrible, desperate struggle for breath. Just one more breath. Just one. But there had been no air and the pain of the water he had sucked into his lungs had raced into every fiber of his body. His head had screamed in agony and his body had writhed and almost burst with the effort to find air.

How long had he struggled? Perhaps it had been even less than a minute. But it had been a minute centuries long. Centuries of terror and pain.

And then his fingers had touched the wooden ladder to the dock and he had clutched it frantically. He had pulled himself up the rungs until he broke the surface of the water. He had hung there, choking and retching, the water spurting from his nose, his head electric with pain. And finally he had been able to get the strength to crawl onto the dock. He had lain there for a long time.

It had been so desolately cold and he had shivered uncontrollably. When he finally sat up, he had looked up at the sky and told it that when the time came for him to die, he would not let it be by drowning. It could be anything else in the world, but it would not be by drowning.

Now Henry looked back at the island again. He could no longer see a flashlight. Noblody was watching him anymore. He had been lost in the darkness.

Henry changed from the crawl to the breast stroke. His head was out of the water now. His heart still pounded wildly. Nothing had gotten any better.

Henry's mind went back to his first day in high school. His freshman year. One of the teachers had helped him fill out his class schedule.

"Can you swim?"

Henry's throat had tightened. "No."

"Then we'll put you down for Beginners' Swimming. Every student here is required to learn to swim before he graduates."

Henry's hands had turned cold. "I'll be here four years, won't I? I mean what's the big rush about swimming? I'd like to take regular gym or something like that first. I'm pretty good at tumbling and gymnastics."

The teacher had shrugged. "All right, Henry. We'll let you take gym this sememster. But I'd advise you to get that swimming requirement out of the way before you hit your senior year. Some students keep putting it off and off, you know."

Henry had begun having nightmares about being in a swimming class. In his dreams he had finally had to report to the swimming instructor at the deep end of the pool. He had stood there, terrified, everybody watching him, wanting for him to jump in. In his dream, he had usually fainted. But even unconscious, he could still hear them laughing.

He had put off taking swimming class until the last semester. But as it approached, he had realized that he was going to have to take swimming. He wouldn't be allowed to graduate without it.

He had gone to the public library and taken out a book on learning how to swim. He had read it over and over until he had just about memorized it.

Then he had gone to a public swimming pool.

The place had been filled with dozens and dozens of kids, screaming and running around the edges of the rectangular pool and jumping in with great big splashes.

He had watched them and then finally he had lowered himself into the shallow end of the pool. The water had been only waist deep, but even then he had trembled. He had edged along the side of the pool until the water reached halfway up his chest. That was far enough.

He had crouched so that the water had come to his chin and then he had practiced breathing the way the book had instructed him. Air in through the mouth, out through the nose.

After a long while, he had pushed off for the opposite end of the pool with the breast stroke that he had studied over and over again.

And he could swim.

It had been like a miracle, swimming back and forth in the shallow water. He could swim. Really swim. His

139

feet had never touched the bottom at all.

He had climbed out and walked down to the deep end of the pool.

And then it had begun. That coldness and terror as he stared down at the light blue water.

No, he had told himself. No. I'm not ready for deep water yet. I've got to get better. A lot better. I've got to practice and practice before I take chances.

He had gone back to the same pool almost every day for the next two weeks and practiced in the shallow water.

Finally he couldn't put it off any longer. He had gone down to the deep end of the pool again. He had climbed down the ladder in the corner of the pool. He had clung there, his heart pounding wildly.

Should he just be brave and push off? But suppose something happened? The pool was crowded. Suppose someone dived right on top of him? Or just bumped him? Would that throw him off? Would he sink to the bottom, gasping, fighting for air?

He had clung to the ladder for nearly ten minutes before he had taken a deep breath, closed his eyes and shoved off.

He had nearly panicked as his feet left the security of the ladder and he had stroked desperately, his eyes shut tight, and holding his breath.

It had come as a surprise, almost a shock, when his fingers touched the opposite side of the pool. He had opened his eyes and grabbed wildly for the rung of the ladder to his right.

His heart had still beaten wildly, but now there had also been jubilation. He had done it!

Quickly, before he could lose his nerve, he had pushed off again and this time half way across he had opened his eyes. On the third lap, he kept his eyes open all the way and even exhaled and took a breath.

He had crossed and recrossed the pool. He had even been bumped into and not panicked. He could swim.

He had kept that fact a secret from everybody. And when his last sememster in high school had begun, he had signed up for Beginners Swimming without even being nervous about it.

Now Henry treaded water, riding the slow sea. There was nothing but darkness from the island now.

I've always been afraid, Henry thought. Not just of the water. But of everything. Except tigers.

Henry could have been valedictorian of his high school class. He had straight A's right up to his last sememster. He had even worked on the speech he would make until he knew every single word by heart. Even today he would sometimes recite the whole thing and wake up sweating.

But Henry had never given his speech. It had come to him slowly but surely that he just couldn't get up there and face all those people staring at him and wondering who he was anyway. All of his classmates and their parents would be wondering when the whole stupid ceremony and the dull speech would end.

Henry had known that Shirley Atkins also had straight A's, except for her class in gym. She probably could become valedictorian and give the speech, if it weren't for him ahead of her.

So Henry had goofed off just enough the last semester so that he had gotten B's in solid geometry and biology II, instead of the usual A's. He had been surprised when he found that he had gotten an A in swimming and he had worried what that might do to raise his average. But luckily, Shirley beat him out by a tenth of a percentage point and she became the valedictorian.

The graduation ceremony had taken place outdoors and while Shirley was giving her speech, Henry had watched a small airplane way up high in the sky.

He had seen something fall from the plane. Or jump. He had thought maybe it's somebody committing suicide. He had watched it fall and then he had seen the parachute open. He had watched the jumper come down slowly and disappear behind some trees.

And Henry had thought, that's probably what I'd be most afraid to do in the whole world. Jump out of an airplane.

That was before he'd tried to swim across Cedar Lake

and learned the real truth about his swimming.

But if I did jump, he had thought, then I would never be afraid of jumping again. Ever. Because I had done the thing I was most afraid of and conquered fear.

Henry had decided then and there that he would enroll in a parachute jumping school. They taught you all the things you needed to know and then you made your first jump.

That night he had had all kinds of nightmares about falling in space and the earth coming closer and closer and the parachute not opening. He had jerked awake a half dozen times, his heart pounding so loud he could hear it.

He wouldn't be able to do it, he had told himself. Jump from an airplane and the whole class watching. He'd be one of those who freezes at the door. He would just stand there, his hands gripping the doorway and nothing could make him jump. Nothing.

But then he had felt a spark of hope. Maybe if he played it slow? Like with the swimming? If he did it his own way, at his own pace....

In the morning, Henry had looked through the yellow pages of the phone book and found the address of one of the parachute jumping schools. He had borrowed Laurie's car and driven out there.

At the airport, he had gone into the office and told the girl behind the counter that he wanted to register for the parachute jumping course and she had handed him a registration form.

Henry had used a fictitious name and invented an address. He had worried a little that she might ask him for a birth certificate or want to see his driver's license for identification, but she hadn't.

"How long will the course take?" he had asked. "I mean how long before I make my first jump?"

"The course starts this weekend. Saturday and Sunday. You jump on the third weekend."

Henry had been surprised that it would be so soon. "Is it possible to buy a parachute here?"

"The school provides the chutes."

"I know. But I still would like to have one of my own."

She had sent him on to the airport manager and when Henry left, he owned a parachute. He stored it in the trunk of the car.

Henry had come back that Saturday and Sunday and the Saturday and Sunday following. He had listened carefully to his instructor and made notes and done all of the things that he was taught to do.

But on the third weekend, he hadn't come back. Instead, he had driven to another airport.

In the small office, he had approached a man in a billed cap who leaned on the counter reading a newspaper. "Do you take people up?" Henry had asked. "I mean like on sightseeing trips and things like that?"

The man had nodded, his eyes on the parachute Henry had slung over one shoulder. "You figuring on jumping?"

Henry had laughed nervously. "No. It's just that my mother says that I've got to wear a chute or I don't go up. You know how mothers are."

When they had stolled out to the Cessna 180, Henry had tried to be casual and make small talk, but he had stopped when he realized that his voice was high and might break.

He had slipped into the parachute and checked the harness with damp fingers. Just getting into a plane itself had always frightened Henry. He had always dreaded those plane flights up to the lake.

Henry had closed his eyes as the plane taxied into position and moved into the takeoff. Once they were up there in the sky, he would just tell the pilot that he had decided to jump after all.

But suppose after he told the pilot that he was going to jump--and then at the very last second--he lost his nerve and didn't? What would the pilot think of him? That he was a coward?

Henry had been in a cold sweat.

No. He wouldn't tell the pilot anything. He would just wait until they were at their peak altitude and then he would jerk open the door and step out before the pilot knew what was happening.

Henry had experienced trouble breathing, as he always did when he was terrified. He had looked out of the plane's side window.

Suppose the chute didn't open? That could happen. It had been in the trunk of the car for three weeks. Suppose he passed out from fright after he jumped? And just fell and fell and regained consciousness when it was too late to pull the rip cord? Or suppose he never regained consciousness at all?

He had begun to tremble violently and he had become aware of the pilot staring at him.

"Something wrong? You look white as a sheet."

Henry had let go of the door handle. "I guess it's just something I ate."

He had closed his eyes. He wasn't going to jump.

When they landed, Henry had driven to the first bar he found down the highway and ordered a martini.

The bartender had asked for some kind of identification and Henry had shown him his driver's license. Henry had been eighteen three days before and so the bartender had shrugged and made him the drink.

Henry had finished the first martini he had ever tasted and then ordered another one.

After a while, he had begun to feel better. Much better. He wasn't shaking anymore and looking at his reflection in the bar mirror, he saw that the color had come back into his face.

The first jump. Yes, that was it. The big hurdle. Make that first jumpa and the rest of them would come easy.

He had ordered a third martini. He could do it. Sure, he could. Take the bull by the horns. Be a man.

Henry finished the third martini and bought a pint of whiskey before he returned to the car.

He had driven ten miles before he had found another airport. Two Piper Cubs were staked down in front of the single hangar.

Henry had opened the pint bottle and managed to keep down a good-sized swallow. Then he had put the bottle back into the glove compartment. He had slung the parachute over his shoulder and walked carefully over to a pair of middle-aged men standing at a gas pump talking.

Henry had meant to ask them if he could rent a plane to take him up, but then suddenly he was sweating again. He had felt cold, and lost, and he knew that he wasn't ever going to make a parachute jump. Not now or ever. There just wasn't enough liquor in the world to make him do it.

Henry had turned on his heel and walked back to the car.

He had driven about a mile and then pulled off onto the shoulder of the road. He had gotten the car door open just in time and then he had been sick.

He had wiped his mouth with a handkerchief and closed the door.

He had begun to cry.

twenty

Oriana had been awake, listening to the night sounds--the bull frogs, the crickets, the languid sweep of wind through the trees outside.

And then there was silence. Even the wind seemed to pause.

Oriana sat up. She waited a few moments and then got out of bed. She went to the closed French windows and looked down at the gardens below.

Henry stepped into the moonlight. Henry still in his swimming trunks. He walked slowly, painfully. He stopped, looked up at the house, and then sat wearily on a garden bench.

Oriana slipped into her dressing gown and sandals. She hurried down the back veranda stairs.

Henry looked up. "Oriana?"

"Yes, Henry."

Henry sighed. "He's not here."

"Who's not here, Henry?"

His face appeared white and haggard. "The tiger. I've been around and around the house, but he's just not here."

"You look very tired, Henry."

"Yes, I'm tired. Very tired." He sighed again. "I came back. I didn't swim to the mainland."

"Yes, Henry. I can see that."

Henry's thin shoulders sagged. "I can really swim a long, long time, Oriana. I can swim for hours and hours. I don't know how many miles I can swim if I really want to.''

"Yes, Henry.''

He was silent for a few moments. "Tonight I swam out about a quarter of a mile. Maybe even less. Maybe a lot less. But then I just couldn't go any farther, Oriana. Not another foot. And I came back.'' He shivered. "I didn't want to drown, Oriana. And I even began worrying about sharks. But mostly drowning.''

Oriana spoke gently. "Why don't you go up to your room, Henry? It's chilly and damp out here.''

Henry wasn't listening. "I nearly drowned when I tried to swim Big Cedar Lake. That was after I didn't make the parachute jump. I never told anybody about that. About the parachute jump or about Big Cedar Lake. I was going to swim across. I wasn't even worried when I started because it's only three miles across the lake and I had done a lot more than that in the high school pool. I swam out about two hundred yards and I saw how much water was still ahead of me. And then when I looked back I thought, suppose I get cramps, I wouldn't even be able to make it back. I panicked, Oriana. And when you panic, you forget how to swim. I would have drowned, but some people in a passing motorboat saw me struggling and pulled me out. And I knew right then that I would never be able to swim across Big Cedar Lake. Or any lake. Not alone.''

He looked at her. "Don't you see, Oriana? My secret. I can swim miles and miles, but that's in a swimming pool. I'm never more than a few feet away from the side. If I get a cramp or get exhausted, I can always make it to the side of the pool. At least that far. I wouldn't drown. And when I swam down the Mississippi nearly a hundred miles, I was never more than fifteen yards from the bank. Ever. If I got into trouble, I knew I could still get to land.''

Henry brushed damp hair from his forehead. "I tried to pretend that Laurie was still alive. I told myself that she was alive and depending on me. I had to save her life by swimming to the mainland, no matter what. But pretending didn't work. I still got terrified and I barely made it back to the island.''

"Why are you looking for the tiger, Henry?"

"Because I'm not afraid of tigers. Not afraid at all. Isn't that strange? I never knew that I'm not afraid of tigers. My whole life, I never knew it. But when I saw the tiger kill Pitts, I suddenly realized something. Tigers are the one thing in the whole world I'm not afraid of. I mean you can't be afraid of everything. It just isn't right. There's got to be something more. And with me, it's tigers. Maybe if I'd known that years ago, it might have helped. But it's too late now. What time is it?"

"A little after midnight. Henry, why don't you go up to your room?"

"No, I'd rather stay out here."

"I'll get you some clothes, Henry. It's too cool to be out here like this."

She hurried up to Henry's room and gathered up the slacks and the shirt Henry had tossed aside when he had changed to swimming trunks. She picked up a pair of his moccasins.

When Oriana returned to the garden, Henry was gone.

"Henry," she called softly. "Henry."

There was no answer.

twenty-one

After MacIntyre left the others, he had hurried back to his room. He gathered up the quilt, the blankets, the pillows, and took them back to the bathroom. He locked the door.

Another tiger. Another damn tiger. Just how many of the filthy animals were there anyway? How had they gotten to the island?

And why hadn't Mike returned by now? What in the world was keeping him? When is he going to get me off this wretched island?

MacIntyre turned off the bathroom light. It was safer in the dark. The tiger might be attracted by light. MacIntyre wiped his damp palms on the quilt.

That damn tiger was out there somewhere. It might even be just outside his bathroom door this very minute.

MacIntyre pulled himself together. No. That couldn't be. After all, he had closed and locked the French doors. If the tiger decided to come in, there would surely be the crash of glass and the splintering of window frames, or something. He giggled nervously. After all, the tiger doesn't have a key. And he can't turn doorknobs.

No, the tiger wasn't out there in the bedroom. Or in anybody else's bedroom. All of their doors would be closed too now that they knew there was at least one more tiger. If a tiger tried to get into anyone's room, there would be noise. Roars, surely. And screams.

Yes, there would be screams. Like Pitt's. Unless somebody else had a weak heart too.

How long had Laurie been dead when MacIntyre had

examined her? Probably not more than two or three minutes. But they would have expected him to do the CPR and maybe she would have begun to come alive again and he would have to keep on....

MacIntyre shivered. No. He couldn't. He just couldn't. And so he had said fifteen minutes. She's been dead fifteen minutes.

He adjusted the pillows. No, the tiger isn't in anybody's room right now. But maybe it was back out there on the veranda? Just sitting there and waiting for one of them to step out?

MacIntyre blinked. The dog.

The dog had chased the tiger away. That ugly little mutt. And Willie always seemed to know when the tiger was near. He at least whined and shivered. And when the tiger came too near, Willie would bark and the tiger would run.

Maybe the dog had so frightened the tiger that it was miles away by now. And even if it returned, Willie would know. He would bark again and the tiger wuld run.

But that changed everything, didn't it? Yes, that made everything quite different.

MacIntyre looked at the luminous dial of his watch. How long would it take before the others got back to sleep again? He would give them a couple of hours. Maybe more.

MacIntyre sat in the darkness, hugging his knees and waiting. The time passed slowly, but it passed.

At two, he got to his feet, unlocked his bathroom door, and peeked out at the semidarkness. Nothing out there. The French doors were still intact.

MacIntyre stepped out of the bathroom. He unlocked one of the doors to the rear veranda and peered out. Nothing. He stepped outside. No light from any of the rooms along the veranda. Good.

MacIntyre walked erect, but as silently as he could down the veranda. He must be quiet, but just in case anyone saw him, he mustn't appear to be sneaking.

MacIntyre moved past Laurie's room and stopped at the end of the veranda. He leaned against the railing and pretended to stare out at the garden.

If any of them had been awake and seen him passing, they might get curious and come out to see what was going on. MacIntyre would say that he hadn't been able to sleep and had come out for some fresh air and he was no longer going to let the tiger run his life.

MacIntyre waited fifteen long minutes. Then five more for insurance. They must all be asleep. Or at least none of them had seen him go by.

MacIntyre moved to the French doors of Laurie's room. He turned the handle slowly. If only that damn dog doesn't bark now. "Willie," he called softly. "Willie."

MacIntyre slipped into the room and closed the door behind him. He locked it.

MacIntyre's eyes searched the moonlit room. Willie wasn't there. One of the others must have taken him.

Laurie's body lay on the bed.

How often he had thought about Laurie. Like that. And he had fantasized. Yes. So many, many times. Sometimes he hadn't really seen the others at all.

Tomorrow Mike would be back. He would come back and send Laurie's body to the mainland. There was just now.

MacIntyre touched Laurie's cold face. He opened her eyes. Yes, the eyes had to be open.

He stared down at her, his heart pounding.

She's dead and I know those eyes are dead. She can't see me. She's dead just like the others. She can't hurt me. She can't laugh. She can't compare. She can't see anything, or do anythng, or expect anything.

MacIntyre slipped out of his bathrobe and pajamas.

He could feel the clammy sweat accumulating on his skin. He began trembling. The trembling became worse. He couldn't control it. He felt as though he was going to burst into a scream of frustration.

The panic swept over him. He snatched his bathrobe and pajamas from the floor, frantically unlocked the door, and fled down the veranda.

In his bathroom he waited until he stopped gasping and then put on his pajamas and bathrobe.

He could have done it. If things had been right. If he hadn't had to worry about the tiger. Or someone looking in and seeing him. He could have done it.

If only he'd brought the camera to the island. Yes, that would have made the difference.

He could have done it. He could have.

He pulled the quilt around him and waited to get warm.

It wasn't fair. It just wasn't fair.

twenty-two

Henry limped through the morning mist. The sand and burrs underfoot had rubbed his bare feet raw and the high underbrush left long red streaks on his torso and legs.

He paused, his eyes searching the ground ahead. The tiger must be here somewhere. Somewhere. Is he running away from me?

Henry moved on. He reached a road--a road leading to a shadowy tunnel created by the live oak branches meeting overhead.

He frowned for a moment in thought. Oh, yes, the road led to the Forrest plantation ruins. Henry had been there once months ago.

He followed the weed-pocketed surface, turned a bend and came upon the station wagon parked on the side of the road. Empty. Just parked there. Who had driven it out here? Probably Pitts.

Henry could drive the car back to the Deveraux house and everyone could get inside and they all would be safe from the tiger.

But the ignition keys were gone. More than likely on Pitt's body, wherever that was now. Could he jump the wires or do something to the ignition to make the car start? No. Henry didn't know anything at all about things like that.

What were those two large jugs on the floor inside? They were filled with a colorless liquid. Water?

Henry could just make out footprints along the side of the road ahead of the car. Pitts had parked the station wagon here for some reason, then gotten out and walked.

Henry peered closer. Really two pairs of tracks. One pair undoubtedly Pitts'. But the other? It was impossible to tell anything except that they were smaller, flat-heeled.

Henry followed the tracks, occasionally losing them in gravel, but picked them up again fifteen or twenty feet ahead. They turned off the road and into the trees.

Deeper tracks in the sandy soil and closer together. It almost seemed as though Pitts had been sneaking up on something.

When Henry reached the clearing at the Forrest plantation, he stopped and stared. Two large cages on wheels, the doors of both of them swinging open.

So the tigers hadn't swum to the island after all? They hadn't escaped from some ship or from some shipwrick? They had been brought in those cages.

Henry approached them. They looked like circus wagon cages and maybe they had been once. Somebody had brought them to the island and towed them all the way inland to the Forrest plantation.

Henry peered into the cages. Water bowls and what looked like the remains of wild pigs. Someone had brought the tigers here and fed them and watered them. Pitts? Was that what those jugs in the station wagon were? Water? And had Pitts shot bush pigs to feed the tigers?

And what had happened?

Had there been some kind of an accident? Had Pitts been drunk and had he accidently let the tiger out?

No. That couldn't be it. Pitts could possibly have made one mistake and one tiger could have escaped. But two cages and each with its own door?

Then what had really happened? Had Pitts been entirely ignorant of the fact that the tigers were loose and was that why he had been killed?

Why would anyone want to let the tigers out of their cages? To kill Pitts? Just Pitts?

Henry walked around the cages.

How many tigers were there really? Had there been only one in each cage? Or two? Were there now three tigers loose? Or just one?

It didn't really matter. He wasn't afraid of tigers. Not all the tigers in the world.

Henry followed one of the sets of tiger tracks and they led him back into the trees. The tracks were probably old, but still they were something to follow and they might lead him somewhere.

Were these the prints of the tiger which had killed Pitts?

Would Henry find his body? Or what was left of it? Whatever he found would have been lying out there two days now. In this climate it would be bloated and stinking.

Henry shivered. He would have to search the remains for the keys to the station wagon. It was his duty. And if he found them, he would have to drive the wagon back to the house.

But the paw prints led toward the Deveraux house, not anywhere near to where Pitts had been killed.

Henry skirted the house, keeping out of sight. He had lost the tiger tracks in the thickening grass, but when he reached the road to the wharf, he decided to follow it, wincing as his feet made contact with the gravel.

Then he stopped.

It's here. Somewhere near. Henry couldn't hear it, or see it, but he knew it was near.

He stepped off the road and into the underbrush, his arms warding off the low branches of the scrub trees.

He saw the tiger.

It lay directly ahead, staring at him.

Henry smiled. Well, tiger, we meet.

Henry walked to within fifteen feet of the animal. The tiger rose to its feet.

Henry turned his back to the tiger and sat down cross-legged. He took off his glasses and put them on the ground beside him.

He stared at the blur ahead. Now, his mind commanded.

Now. Now. Now.

The tiger sprang and it was over in a moment.

It sniffed at Henry's body and then backed off. It

stared and retreated farther. Then it abruptly turned and ran.

It sped through the underbrush and onto the road. It ran until it reached the ocean and it stopped there, panting. It looked back, still puzzled.

The tiger turned to the sea. It saw something out there on the water. Something coming nearer and making noise.

The tiger backed into the underbush to watch and wait.

twenty-three

Mike shaded his eyes. Another ten minutes and he'd hit the island.

He was feeling better now. The whiskey was working and so were the four aspirins.

Hell, he'd been drinking too much the last few days, but what else was there to do when you're just waiting.

He had left the island late Tuesday night. On the mainland he'd phoned for the taxi from Anchor Sam's and checked in at a hotel in Savannah. He'd put in a few hours of sleep and then met with Mecklemann and his boys.

Mecklemann directed the Fergusson Construction legal department and Mike had told him to come down here and look at the whole deal.

Mecklemann had brought along people who knew about property and development and all that crap and Mike had left it all to them.

They had even been to the island a couple of weeks ago. Not that they really needed to see the place at all. What they were interested in were facts and figures and most of those were with the banks and lawyers in Savannah.

Mecklemann had come right down to the nitty-gritty of it. He had told Mike that he'd better forget about buying the whole island and trying to develop it. It was just too big a deal for one man to swing these days. Mike didn't have that kind of loose money, even if he did own Fergusson Construction. If Mike still wanted to go ahead with the deal, he'd have to bring in outside money and a lot of it. And that meant that Mike would probably lose control of the operation.

Hell, Mike had been relieved. Yes, damn relieved. It had been a wild thing to begin with. He'd just jumped at the idea without thinking. Maybe he'd known all along that he wasn't really going to go through with it. He'd just brought the experts down so that they could talk him out of it.

What he owned on the island was more than enough for what he had in mind now--the Deveraux place and a couple of dozen of acres around it. Let the island stay the way it was. Quiet and deserted. He'd still have the run of the place and that was all he really wanted.

After the meeting, Mike had taken a taxi back to Anchor Sam's. It had been raining like hell and it looked like it was never going stop. There wasn't a chance of getting back to the island. The sea had been heavy and practically no visibility.

So Mike had sat in the barroom hoping that some broad might come cruising in, but it had been a dead day. That night he'd rented a room from Anchor Sam and gone upstairs with a bottle.

He had opened his eyes early the next morning feeling like hell. The weather had looked like it was going to be just like the day before and he'd been damned if he was going to spend all day and maybe another night at Anchor Sam's. So he had taken a couple of shots from the bottle, phoned for a taxi, and headed back to Savannah.

He'd stopped off at Randall's Sporting Goods and found that the Weatherby .378 Magnum he'd ordered had come in. Mike also picked up ammunition, some for the other Weatherby. He'd used all he had on the island on target practice and shooting those pigs.

According to Pitts, the tigers didn't care much for pig meat. Probably hated the fishy taste. They were almost ready to starve before they'd take a bite. So Mike had decided he'd better get them horse meat. You sure couldn't feed the cats steaks and chops.

Mike had bought a chest type freezer and had it shipped to the island, but getting horse meat wasn't that easy. Finally Mike had found a place in Savannah and the first shipment of horse meat was due in a few days.

Nobody but Mike and Pitts knew about the tigers. Not even Oriana. He'd done all of the paper work himself. If word about the cats got out or what he meant to do with them, there might be bleeding hearts on the mainland who'd try to stop him. And besides, he wanted to try the whole thing on his own before he told anybody else.

Yes, he'd sure have to keep the tigers a secret from Forrest, especially now that the deal was off. Forrest might not like th idea of having tigers running around his half of the island.

After Mike had left the sports shop, he'd seen that the day had cleared up after all. But he'd been hungry and so he'd gone to a restaurant. After a steak, he'd decided he could use a drink, and so he'd gone to a bar, still carrying the cased rifle.

That was where he'd picked up Mary Lou, in the cocktail lounge. Turned out that she was some kind of a computer operator, this was her day off, and she was looking for the same thing he was.

They had spent the afternoon drinking and then gotten a hotel room.

He had fallen asleep after, or maybe just passed out. He woke early this morning just as it was beginning to get light. The skies were clear, and it had been time to get back to the island.

He had felt like hell, so he had forced down a couple of drinks. When he had left, Mary Lou had still been sleeping.

He had taken a taxi back to Anchor Sam's, downed a few more drinks, taken some aspirins and shoved off for the island.

Now he cut the throttle and let the boat glide in toward the dock. He'd hoped that somebody might be there waiting--it was always tricky trying to moor a boat alone-- but the wharf was deserted.

There was something attached to one of the pilings. It looked like a picture frame.

After Mike secured the aft and bow lines, he read the note behind the glass.

He swore. Damn Pitts. He probably got drunk and let one of the tigers escape. And now it was out there scaring the hell out of everybody.

Mike returned to the cruiser's cabin and uncased the Weatherby. He slipped cartridges into the magazine clip and a few more into his pockets.

He stepped off the boat and began walking down the wharf.

twenty-four

Mike went to the liquor cabinet and fixed himself a drink.

Lord what a day.

So all hell had broken loose while he was off the island. How had it happened? Had Pitts gotten so drunk that he thought it would be fun to turn the tigers loose? If he had, he didn't have much of a chance to laugh.

The tiger.

Mike smiled. God that had been it! The tops!

The big cat had come bounding out of the brush and he'd just had time to bring up the rifle. It had been close.

The damn tiger must have died right in midair. The bullet had smashed its brain to a pulp. The cat had jerked like it was tearing itself in half and then it had slammed to the ground and skidded a couple of yards on its back. Cats always land on their feet. But not dead cats.

God, what a wonderful feeling. To kill the animal and stand there looking down at it right at your feet. He'd been tempted to smear some of the blood on his face.

Mike could buy more tigers. But why stop with tigers? You could get almost any animal these days. But he'd have to be careful about that, especially from now on.

Mike took a swallow from his glass.

He had killed the tiger, then walked on to the house where he had found out what had happened while he was gone. But hell, he still didn't really know everything.

He'd had to go back to the mainland for the police and they'd sent men to search for Pitts' body. They'd also found Henry, and the Bowlers.

Mike still couldn't figure out what had happened with Henry. According to Oriana he had tried to swim to the mainland, but then he'd gotten a cramp and just made it back. She said that they'd better search the island because he might be wandering out there sick.

They had found his body. Neck broken, but hardly any other mark on him.

The police had wanted to know how the tigers and the cages had gotten onto the island. Mike had told them that he was damned if he knew. He didn't have the faintest idea. It was a big island and he owned only a small piece of it.

They'd had to buy that. Pitts was the only one who could have told them different, and he was dead.

And the Bowlers. What the hell had happened there? They'd found what was left of Bowler. And his wife lying there wrapped up in a canvas tarp. Nobody could figure out how she had really died.

And Laurie dead too.

Well, it was bound to happen, sooner or later. Mike hoped that nobody had noticed that he hadn't rushed up there to see her body.

Hell, what was the point in looking at dead bodies? Dead human bodies? Once a person is dead, that's it. Why stare at dead meat. Or touch it. When you're dead, you're dead, and you ought to be carted away.

God, he remembered those damn funerals when he was a kid. It seemed like some relative was always dying and his mother would drag him to the funeral and those stinking viewings.

You'd sit in those folding chairs and stare at the prettied-up corpse. Mike would watch for any movement. Like breathing, or a twitch, and he had always been afraid that the body would sit up and come walking slowly toward him with eyes staring from hell.

He remembered the two bodies Jamie had shown him when they were kids, both about twelve or thirteen years old. Jamie had dared him to come into the basement of the funeral parlor.

Mike had said what the hell would I want to see a

dead body for? And Jamie said, I guess not, if you're afraid?

So Jamie had sneaked Mike in the back way of MacIntyre's funeral parlor and they had gone down to the basement.

Jamie had switched on the lights and there they were. Two naked bodies on their backs and the woman's eyes open. They had looked like wax except that you knew damn well they weren't. Mike had said, so there's two bodies lying there. Big deal.

Jamie had said, don't you want to touch them?

And Mike had said, what is the big deal about touching dead bodies? Only creeps touch dead bodies and I'm not a creep. Like you.

Then Mike had put a fist under Jamie's nose and said if you ever lie to anybody that I'm afraid to touch a dead body, I'll kick your balls up your throat.

Jamie had gotten white and promised that he wouldn't and crossed his heart.

Mike still had nightmares about those damn bodies. They would sit up, their eyes big and dark, and they would come after him moaning.

Mike finished his drink and made another.

He'd had all of the bodies taken off the island. Except for Pitts. He would be buried here. Why give the bastard an expensive funeral?

Life and death. That's the way it went. Some live and some die. It was in the cards or it wasn't.

He could just as well have been on that plane when old man Fergusson cashed in. If it hadn't been for the flu, he would have been inside when it crashed. That had been an accident, not that he hadn't wished it pretty often.

But with Myra, it had been different.

He'd watched her standing out there in the moonlight at the end of the dock, looking up at the stars and thinking whatever it was that dum-dums think.

And he'd thought, hell, I'm not going to have her around my neck for the rest of my life. So he'd gotten into his slippers and walked out there as quietly as he could.

She had probably never even heard him. He had just given her a shove and in she went. She hadn't come up even once. Then he'd gone back to the cabin and gotten some sleep.

Mike stared at himself in the mirror. I've got to cut down on the drinking. It's beginning to show.

How long should he wait before he talked to Eve? Did she know how he really felt about her?

He'd never said anything. He'd never tried anything. Nothing at all. Always kept his hands off and respected her and her person. She was something real different. Not like the millions of broads out there.

Somehow she reminded him of somebody. Or something. It always made him feel a little uneasy because he couldn't quite put his finger on who or what it was. Might even be some statue.

Her eyes. There was something about her eyes. They seemed to stop you right in your tracks.

Yes, he'd wait about a year and then he'd tell Eve how he really felt about her and ask her to marry him.

He looked into the mirror again. Suppose she said no?

twenty-five

Oriana emptied the contents of the plastic container onto her night table.

The night Forrest had come to the island, she had slept fitfully. Why couldn't he have conducted the entire business by mail? Why did he have to come back here at all?

Suppose he decided not to sell his part of the island? But what good could the Forrest plantation be to him now? The overgrown land, the ruins, they could mean nothing to him.

She had sighed. But perhaps they did. Perhaps we, the last two island people in the world, are the only ones left in the world who care.

She had shivered. No, they weren't the last island people. There was Pitts.

When Oriana learned that Mike had hired Pitts as his caretaker, she had been horrified. She had gone to Mike immediately and asked him to get rid of Pitts.

Mike had been mildly surprised. "What's wrong with Pitts?"

"He's undependable and he drinks."

"Hell, I know he drinks. I do a little of that myself. But you'd be surprised how hard it is to get anybody to stay on the island the whole year around. All I really need is his body out there, I don't expect a lot of work out of him. How do you know he drinks? Ever meet the man in person?"

Oriana had been reluctant to admit that much. "Yes. When he was the caretaker at the Forrest plantation.

Until the place burnt down and he could have been responsible for that."

"You told me the house was hit by lightning."

"Yes, it was. I meant that there might have been something that Pitts could have done when the fire first started. But he was probably dead drunk."

"Why didn't he burn up with the house?"

"He preferred to sleep in one of the slave cabins out back."

"Is there anything else you know about Pitts?"

Oriana had hesitated. Mike was getting too curious. Even if she did get him to fire Pitts, was Pitts the kind of a man who would just go away? Or would he make trouble?

Yes, she had thought, he would probably make trouble that could change the relationship between her and Mike entirely. And so Oriana had decided not to say anything more about Pitts. She would have to find some other way to get rid of him.

The morning after Forrest had come to the island, Oriana had gotten up at dawn.

She had gone down the back stairs, through the old garden, and walked once again to the Forrest plantation. There had been fog, but it had been patchy at ground level and she had had no trouble finding her way.

Oriana hadn't been to the Forrest plantation since the last time they had all come to the island nearly two months before. But whenever she was here, she would slip quietly away, sometimes even at night. She would take the old path to the plantation and she would almost expect to see the Forrest house again as it had been when she was a girl.

But the house was gone, of course, and so she would just stand in the ruins and dream of what it would look like again some day.

That morning as she approached the Forrest plantation, she had seen something new, and different, and startling--the two large cages under the live oaks. She had approached wide-eyed and seen what was inside of them.

Tigers. One in each cage.

166

And then she had remembered Mike coming back to the office late one afternoon after a lunch with county zoo executives.

He had sat down at his desk, his voice slurring, probably because of martinis. "Oriana, did you know that the tiger is an endangered species?"

Oriana had said yes, she supposed so.

Mike had nodded. "But only in the wild, Oriana. In the zoos he's not an endangered species at all. The simple fact is that tigers are breeding like crazy in captivity. We've got tigers and tigers. We're knee deep in tigers and the zoos don't know what to do with them all. And so they're selling tigers. Not just to other zoos or circuses, but to anybody with the money. Oriana, I can buy myself a tiger if I feel like it."

"What would you do with a tiger, Mike?"

He had grinned. "I'd shoot it."

Mike had said no more about tigers after that day, but she saw now that he had been serious about buying them. Yes, now he had two tigers and he was probably going to shoot them. He would invite some of his friends to the island, let the tigers out of their cages, and there would be a tiger hunt.

It was a pity really, Oriana had thought. They looked quite beautiful.

She had sat down on one of the fallen columns in the ruins. She couldn't remember how long she had been there dreaming, but then she had heard the sound of careful footsteps. She had turned to look behind her.

It had been Pitts.

He had been almost crouching as he approached, his arms dangling, and he'd had that look in his eyes again.

He had smiled, showing yellowed teeth. "I saw you leave the house this morning and I wondered where the hell you'd be going this early. I took a guess and here I am."

He had moved closer. In another moment she would have smelled him and his breath.

Oriana had stood up and backed away until her shoulders touched one of the tiger cages. She had looked up, seen the cage latch, and reached up. She had grasped the handle and pulled as hard as she could. The cage door had swung open. She had turned back to Pitts.

He had stopped, his mouth open, his face whitening. "You damn fool!" He had backed slowly away from her and the cage. Then he had turned and begun to run.

The tiger had come to the open doorway of its cage and looked down at her. Then its attention had been attracted by the sight of Pitts running.

It had leaped gracefully from the cage and begun loping after Pitts. The tiger seemed to be in no hurry. It had almost appeared as though it were herding Pitts toward Thompson's Hill.

Oriana had run all the way back to the Deveraux house. She had almost reached it when she heard Pitts scream. She had looked back and seen the tiger standing over his body.

Forrest and MacIntyre had been in the garden staring at the tiger, and she had seen Henry on the second floor veranda, but she had avoided them all by keeping to the trees and entering the house from the front.

She had, of course, been stunned by what had happened. Should she tell the others that she was responsible for freeing the tiger? And should she tell them why? But what difference would that really make? It would change nothing. The tiger had killed Pitts. That couldn't be undone and Oriana hadn't felt at all as though she were a cold-blooded murderess. Releasing the tiger had been a necessity. Pitts' death hadn't been planned. It had almost been an accident.

Yes, it would be best to keep quiet about everything. Now that everyone knew that there was a tiger loose on the island, they could simply take the precaution of remaining in the house. And if the animal actually threatened them, there was always Mike's rifle. No one was in any real danger.

But it hadn't been until the next morning that Laurie had found the cartridge for the Weatherby and Forrest had shot the tiger.

It had been a tense period of waiting for Oriana, but now it was all done with, she had thought. She wouldn't ever have to tell anyone how the tiger had gotten out of its cage.

That night there had been another tiger.

How had it gotten out of its cage? Oriana had wondered. Did Henry have anything to do with that? He seemed to find some strange fascination in tigers. Had he discovered the cages too and released the second tiger?

Mike had finally come back to the island this morning and killed the second tiger as it sprang at him at the base of the wharf.

When he reached the house, they had told Mike about Laurie and Pitts. They hadn't known at the time what had happened to Henry or the Bowlers.

Mike had returned to the mainland to notify the authorities. His cruiser, and several others, had returned to the island. There had been police, newspapersmen, the search parties, and others who had just been curious.

It had been a long day. There had been the questioning and the search of the island. They had found the Bowlers first, just behind the last slave cabin. And Pitts. And finally Henry.

It had been evening before Mike had talked to Oriana alone. "Oriana, that does it. I've decided to forget about the whole damn project."

Oriana had not really been surprised. "Forget about the project?"

"This whole damn island, Oriana. The place is a jinx. I mean Laurie dead. And Henry. There's nothing here for me but bad luck and bad memories."

Mike's face had been flushed with drink. "The whole thing was crazy anyway, Oriana. What the hell do I know about real estate development? I could lose my shirt. Besides, Eve doesn't care for the island at all."

Oriana had smiled faintly. That was the important thing now? Eve doesn't like the island?

"I'll keep the Deveraux house, of course. I know how much it means to you. We'll sneak down here every once in a while. Just the two of us. Let the banks and Forrest keep their part of the damn island. I'll just borrow it now and then when I need the exercise."

Mike had smiled. "I don't see how what's happened here should change anything between us, Oriana, except that we probably won't have you with us on weekends so often now."

Ah, yes, Oriana had thought tiredly. We.

"But I'll still see you as often as I can. I mean you would still keep the apartment. I'd see to that."

Oriana had sighed. That was the way it was going to be? She would still remain his mistress, but there would be no Forrest Plantation rising from the ashes. All she had done had really been for nothing. Nothing at all.

And yet had she really been surprised? I'm sorry, Laurie, she had thought, but it just didn't work out the way you meant it to be.

When Oriana left Mike, she had almost bumped into Forrest and MacIntyre.

She had stared at Forrest. Why not you? Why not you? Suppose I smiled and did my damndest to be nice?

She had seen herself in the wall mirror behind him-- her face white, her eyes wide, and she had thought, My God, what have I become?

She had turned from them and hurried upstairs to MacIntyre's room.

In the past, when Oriana had not been able to sleep, MacIntyre would give her some capsules and she remembered that he had always gotten them from a plastic container in the top drawer of his dresser.

She entered his room and pulled open the drawer. Yes, they were there. She had expected them to be. MacIntyre was a methodical man.

Oriana took the container to her room and emptied it on her night table. She counted the capsules. Twenty-six. When MacIntyre had given her only two, she had slept nearly nine hours.

Oriana changed into her nightgown and brushed her hair. She got a glass of water from the bathroom.

She put two of the capsules into her mouth, sipped water, and swallowed.

She was tired. So tired.

It's all going to be over soon. It's going to end at last.

She reached for two more capsules.

170

twenty-six

Forrest watched Oriana pick up the second pair of capsules. He tapped on one of the French door panes.

Oriana quickly dropped a handkerchief over the capsules. "Who is it?"

"Forrest." He did not wait for an invitation to enter, but stepped inside. He went directly to the nightstand and lifted the handkerchief. "I don't know what's inside of these things, but do you really intend taking them all?"

"Have you been out there watching?"

"Discreetly. When you brushed past me downstairs, you had that wild look about you. I don't exactly read minds, but I thought it might be a good idea to see what you intended to do next. I watched you go into MacIntyre's room and come out clutching that little bottle."

"This is really none of your business."

"I suppose not." Forrest took a chair facing her. "I was going to speak to you tomorrow, but now I see that might be too late."

Oriana waited.

"If you've got your mind made up about this grand gesture, I don't intend to stop you." He studied her for a few moments. "Since we seem to be short on time, I might as well be blunt. First, I gather that you are Mike's mistress?"

She colored faintly. "Everyone knows that. Why should you be an exception?"

He nodded. "And since I have never seen that suicidal gleam in your eyes before, I very cleverly deduce that it is there because of something that Mike just told you? Or

171

didn't tell you?"

"I would appreciate it if you left."

"Let me leap to another brilliant conclusion. You had great expectations of a promotion now that Laurie is dead, but you found out that it isn't going to happen?" He smiled. "Mike doesn't strike me as being all that desperately lovable, though I could be wrong, of course. Was it really his money you were after?"

Oriana glared at him. "Of course it was his money. That's it exactly. Now go."

Forrest nodded. "But there are limits as to how much of his money you can expect as his mistress? Therefore you had to become his wife? What do you want with all of his money anyway?"

Oriana closed her eyes for a moment. "Very well, if your happiness depends on knowing, I had glorious hopes of rebuilding the Forrest plantation, and that would take a lot of money."

Forrest raised an eyebrow. "You would rebuild my house?"

"I never thought of it as your house. Or anybody else's. It was mine."

"But now all hope is ended? How easily you give up."

"Easily?"

"Of course. Now that Mike is out of the picture, it seems perfectly obvious to me what your next step should be. After all, I am here and I do still own the important half of this island. I have quite a lot of money and I think of you rather favorably."

Oriana stared. "All right then, damn it, would you rebuild the Forrest plantation if I asked you to?"

"No." Forrest smiled. "I wouldn't rebuild that house because it's the wrong thing to do. It's a time over and done with. You can't bring it back and you shouldn't. And besides, I don't think this island is all the happy memories you want to think it is."

He glanced at the night table again. "Oriana, I have the strong suspicion that you are a nicer person than you think you are. I also have the feeling that you aren't ending it all simply because Mike turned you down. You're taking those capsules because you're tired of the whole damn road and nothing looks better for tomorrow. Have you ever been to Pennsylvania?"

Oriana blinked. "Pennsylvania?"

"Yes. It has four seasons, you know. You'd like them, except for February, which nobody can stand. By that time you're tired of the snow, but you'll love it in December and January. Someday I'll tell you about the Baron and Pitot sisters."

Oriana sighed. "Oh, Lord."

"They lived on this island a long, long time ago and then moved to Pennsylvania where they bought a farm. It's mine now. I traced them down for the hell of it and liked the place. I've got the Baron's flute and the Pitot sisters' harp and harpsichord. I think you might enjoy learning to play either the harp or the harpsichord. You have your choice. However I must warn you that you'd be required to practice at least one hour a day. Possibly two."

"You're crazy."

Forrest agreed. "Actually I think it's something I caught from Henry. Maybe it's just what we need at a time like this."

He got to his feet. "I guess that's about all I have to say. Think it over. Will I see you in the morning?"

Oriana looked away, her eyes thoughtful.

When he was gone, she sighed and swept the capsules into the wastebasket.

She was asleep when a faint smile came to her lips.

Harpsichord.

twenty-seven

Eve stepped out onto the veranda.

What had really happened out there at the cages? Had the first tiger accidently escaped while Pitts had been feeding it or cleaning its cage?

Eve had known about the tigers, of course, but she hadn't known that Mike had shipped them to the island.

She had been going through his papers at the office--as she usually did after Mike and Oriana had left for the day--to see if there was anything important she ought to know and remember. She had found the bill of sale for the two tigers and the two cages, and she had wondered what the hell is this?

She could have asked Mike, but then he would have known she had a key to that particular drawer and that she had been going through his things. So she had just waited for Mike to tell her all about the tigers, but he never had.

They had evidently been Mike's little secret and he had not wanted anyone else to know about them. Not Oriana, not Laurie, not anyone. Except Pitts, probably. Mike needed someone to take care of the animals and Pitts was to keep his mouth shut.

Why had Mike shipped them to the island? She had guessed that he intended to turn them loose and hunt them down. Mike was a great one for hunting and he'd never shot a tiger before.

Yes. one of the tigers had gotten loose and at the house they had found that there was no ammunition for Mike's rifle.

174

Eve had remembered that Mike also owned a revolver, a .357 Magnum. He had shown it to her and said that he had bought it in Savannah.

Eve had waited for someone to mention the existence of the hand gun, but no one had. Evidently Eve was the only one who knew that Mike had it, and he had told her what a powerful weapon it was--that it could destroy an engine black, or something like that--with just one bullet.

It could kill a tiger, Eve had thought. You wouldn't intentionally go tiger hunting with just a handgun, but in an emergency it would do. She had been about to tell Forrest about the Magnum, but she had changed her mind.

There might be a time to kill the tiger, but that time might not be now. No, not just yet. First, she would wait and see.

So she had said nothing about the gun, or that she knew about the tigers, but she had no intention of becoming one of the tiger's victims herself.

When she had the chance, she had let herself into Mike's room and she had found the revolver in a drawer of his bureau. Yes, quite an impressive weapon and there had been a cartridge in every chamber.

Eve would be safe enough if she kept the revolver with her, but how could she carry it? In her shoulder bag? No, one doesn't carry one of those everywhere one goes, especially not inside a house.

Then she had remembered Laurie's knitting. Yes, a knitting bag would be ideal. She could carry that with her everywhere and no one would ask questions.

She had gone to Laurie and told her that she wanted something to do to calm her nerves and she thought that knitting just might do the trick.

Laurie had been suspicious, knowing that there was something not quite right about that. Laurie could see a great deal more than people gave her credit for. But then she had shrugged, given Eve a few instruction on how to begin knitting, and let her use the bag.

Suppose the tiger made an appearance, Eve had wondered, and she were forced to use the gun to protect herself? How would she explain to the others that she had said nothing about the revolver?

She would tell them that she had known that pistols weren't made for killing tigers, and that she had been afraid that if one of the men knew about he revolver, he might have been tempted to do something heroic and go out and try to shoot the animal, and so she had refrained from telling them about the gun. Yes, that would do nicely.

Eve had waited rather hopefully to see what the tiger might do next, but then Laurie had found the single rifle cartridge and Forrest had killed the beast. The first tiger.

Eve had been quietly furious, of course, until she had realized that there were, after all, two tigers and two cages and they had probably both been shipped to the island. Had both of the tigers escaped? Or been let out by someone? Or was one of the tigers still in its cage somewhere on the island.

Yes, but where on the island?

Perhaps it wouldn't be too difficult to find at that. There was only one usable road remaining on the island. Pitts had probably used the missing station wagon to get to the cages. She would simply follow the road.

She had waited until late in the afternoon, then changed to her walking shoes, and slipped out of the house. She had carried the knitting bag with her and she had followed the gravel road inland. After perhaps a mile and a half, she had found the station wagon at the side of the road, its keys still in the ignition.

Pitts had evidently driven the wagon this far and then parked it here. She could see his footprints in the sand at the side of the road and she had followed in their tracks until they turned into a long lane of live oaks.

This had once been the driveway leading to the old Forrest plantation. The footprints had become more difficult to find now, but it appeared that Pitts had for some reason kept close to the trees.

Eve had gone on and finally found the two tiger cages, the door to one of them hanging open. However the other cage still remained secure and inside, in its semi-darkness, she had seen the second tiger.

176

It had stared at her, its eyes blinking, but otherwise unmoving.

Eve had returned to the station wagon, on the way picking up a fallen bare branch which seemed to be just about the right length for what she intended to do next.

She had driven the wagon back to the cages and rolled down a window. She used the branch to force the latch of the tiger's cage upward. The door had creaked open.

Eve had rolled up the window and backed the station wagon from the cages.

The big cat had remained motionless for more than a minute. Then it had risen slowly and moved toward the open cage door, stopping a foot short and sniffing the air suspiciously.

At last it had seemed to gather its courage and it leaped to the ground. It had regarded Eve and the station wagon for a few moments and then had turned and loped into the brush.

Eve had driven back to the point where she had picked up the station wagon, made a U-turn and parked. She had tossed the ignition keys into the brush. She hadn't wanted any of the others finding the car and bringing it back to the house where it might be used as a refuge from the second tiger.

She had hurried back to the Deveraux house, confident that she would get there before the tiger. But, just to be on the safe side, she had kept her hand in the knitting bag.

She had reached the house at dusk. There had been a light in Laurie's room and her French doors had been open to the night air.

Eve had gone up to her own bedroom, closed the doors, and waited.

The tiger would come. It must. It would be attracted to the house by the lights. By the people. After all, it probably hadn't eaten since Pitts died. It must be hungry. Very hungry.

Eve had waited, sitting in the darkness, and it had seemed forever. But at last she had seen the silhouette of the tiger outside. She had watched it pass and then she had waited again. Perhaps for a scream.

But Laurie's dog had begun to bark, and Eve had seen the tiger bounding away in flight.

Damn, she had thought, damn, damn, damn. That filthy little mutt frightened the tiger away. She had felt like shooting Willie. Right then and there. Blasting him into a thousand bits.

The dog had stopped barking and Eve had pulled herself together. She heard Forrest and Henry out on the veranda and she had decided to join them and be as surprised as they that there was another tiger on the island.

And then they had all moved on to Laurie's bedroom and found her dead.

The tiger hadn't touched her. Laurie had evidently died of a heart attack. But how she died didn't matter. Just as long as it was done. Over with. Yes, they had all known about Laurie's heart and Eve had waited and waited for years.

Eve had taken the dog Willie back to her room. She had felt better about Willie. Good dog. She could depend on him to bark if the tiger came back.

She had closed her eyes and gone to sleep.

The next morning, Eve had been about to go down for breakfast when she had heard the faint report of a rifle shot. It had been Mike returning to the island and killing the second tiger.

Dear Laurie, wherever you are, you really knew me, didn't you? You knew what was going to happen after you died if you didn't do something about it. And that's why you brought Oriana into the house--deliberately brought her into the household because you wanted to choose Mike's next wife and you knew she shouldn't be me. You knew me, Laurie. You knew that I would devour Mike.

But it's not going to work, Laurie. Mike won't wait long before he tells me how he feels. He'll be afraid that he'll lose me if he doesn't speak up. And we'll be married, Laurie.

I know what's going to happen, Laurie. Yes, I know exactly what is going to happen.

Mike will drink too much the first night and he will pass out before we even get near a bedroom. And the next morning, he will apologize. But he will drink again the second night and pass out once more. Maybe even the third night before he can think of some excuse for not doing what he thought he had wanted all these years. And what will his excuse be?

He will say something like, I know that it's hard to understand, Eve, but I think it's in my subconscious or something and I have this guilt feeling.

Oh? I will ask so innocently. A guilt feeling?

Yes, he will say. I mean about Laurie and waiting such a short time before getting married again. Somehow that's on my subconscience and I feel that it's wrong not to wait longer. That's why I drink so much and don't...

And I will say, it's all right, Mike, I understand. Let's just wait one full year before we even try to do anything?

Mike will grab at that. Yes, he will say, I think that we should wait a full year. And you're positive you understand, Eve?

Of course, I will say, and we will sleep in separate bedrooms.

Eve smiled faintly. Yes, she had been quite surprised when Mike had offered to adopt her. She had expected some other arrangement. Even after she had moved into Mike's house, she had expected her bedroom door to open and Mike would be standing there. But it had never happened.

It had puzzled her at first, but then gradually she had seen what it really was.

Maybe she reminded him of his sainted mother, or something else sainted and sacred, but whatever it was, it made her oh so different. It made her something you watched, and longed for, but never touched. And when he finally realized that, it would be something he could not face, or live with.

Yes, they would get married.

The months would pass and Mike would drink more and more. There would be nights when he would stop outside her bedroom door and carefully try the knob to see if she had locked herself in. She never would. He would release the knob again, without opening the door. He would stand there for a while, and then perhaps he would knock gently, hoping and not hoping, that she was asleep.

She would ask, what is it? And he would say I thought I heard a noise. Like someone falling, I guess. Are you all right?

And Eve would say, yes, I'm all right. Is there anything else?

He would quickly say no, no, I'm sorry I bothered you, and he would go back to his bottle and drink until he passed out.

Mike would begin drinking when he woke in the morning. When he did get to the office, he would be late, and sometimes he wouldn't show up at all.

But Eve would be at the company every day. Early. And it wouldn't be long before everyone knew who was really running the company. And Mike would begin to realize that too. He would begin to see that he really didn't matter. He was nothing. To the company. To Eve. It would eat into him and he would probably wait until the very last night the year was up.

He would drink, of course, but not too many this time. Just enough to give him the courage. He would pick up the revolver. Perhaps it would even be the .357 Magnum. He would put the barrel to his head and pull the trigger.

Eve would be waiting for the shot and when she heard it, she would send one of the servants to Mike's bedroom.

Everything would belong to her.

She would be somebody. There would be money and power and she would see that both of them grew and grew. She would become important. Looked up to.

Yes, she had known that someday it would happen. It would take hard work, but even more, you couldn't let things just happen. You had to be able to know when to act, to do the right things at the right time.

Eve looked up at the bright stars. The millions and millions of stars.

You died. You died a long time ago, but you've been up there watching me. You've been watching me all these years.

Her eyes gleamed with love and hate and madness.

She smiled.

Well, Daddy, how am I doing now?

180